CHRISTIANS YOU SHOULD KNOW

Lincoln, Nebraska 68501

Published with permission of Moody Press

This book was first published in the
United States by the Moody Press
of the Moody Bible Institute of Chicago.

Back to the Bible Broadcast edition

18,000 printed to date—1980
(5-9068—6M—20)
ISBN 0-8474-1723-9

Printed in the United States of America

Introduction

This is a book of biographies. A biography is a story of the life of a person. It usually tells where and when the person was born, who his parents were, what his home was like and something about the early life of the person.

This type of book is often written for adults and teenagers, but that is not the purpose of this book. This book is written for the younger reader, with the hope that it will help them to know something about these famous men and women of the past, so that when they are older, they will want to study their lives and read more about them.

This book will tell something about missionaries, singers, poets, evangelists and other workers for God. All of them were faithful in His service; all of them were *Christians you should know.*

Contents

John Eliot

John Eliot is best known for his faithful work among the Indians. While some people did not seem to care for the Indians, John Eliot preached the gospel to them, taught them to read and even translated God's Word for them. They learned to trust John Eliot as a dear friend.

John Eliot—Missionary to the Indians

John Eliot is not as well known as some missionaries. He preached mostly to the Indians of Massachusetts. In explaining his purpose, he said it was to "win the natives of the country to the knowledge and obedience of the only true God and Saviour of mankind."

Almost all the people of that day seemed to hate the Indians. In fact, they almost despised them. To the Englishmen who lived in Massachusetts, the Indians were a "human nuisance." Some even considered them as "devils." Cotton Mather said they were "the very ruins of mankind." Roger Williams called them "wolves with brains of men." But not John Eliot. Somehow he felt that they were close to his heart. He knew that the Bible is

7

the true Word of God and that he must be faithful to God and give the gospel of Jesus Christ to these Indians.

To John Eliot these men and women were human beings whom God had created. They were men and women who had souls. They were sinners who needed the Lord Jesus as their Saviour. The more he thought of it, the more convinced he was that these people needed to hear God's Word and accept Christ as their Saviour.

John Eliot was born in Widford, Hertfordshire, England, in 1604. When he was 14, he went to Jesus College in Cambridge, England. He finished his studies there in 1622. After this he became an usher in the Thomas Hooker school. Rev. Thomas Hooker went to America. Because John Eliot thought so much of Mr. Hooker, he followed him there in 1631.

John Eliot loved children—Indian children especially. He was very patient with them. One year after John Eliot arrived in the United States, his friend Anne Mumford also came to join him.

John Eliot's first job was as a substitute in the First Church of Boston. The people there liked him very much, and the elders would have kept him, but John Eliot could only think of his friends who lived in the hilly country. So he and the many people who had followed him from England settled there, and before long the church in Roxbury was established. This was in 1632, ten years after his college work was finished.

John Eliot stayed with these people for more than 50 years.

In 1646 John Eliot started working with the Indians. A young Indian boy by the name of Job

Nesutan became Mr. Eliot's teacher and helper. This Indian boy spoke English perfectly and was able to help John Eliot in learning the Indian language. After they had worked hard for about two years, Mr. Eliot was able to preach to the Indians in their own language. He and Job Nesutan also translated the Ten Commandments and the Lord's Prayer into the Indian language.

Some people made fun of John Eliot. They said it would be better to teach the Indians English than to try to translate the Scriptures into their mixed-up language. But John Eliot did not let that bother him. He knew God had called him to work with these people, so he pressed right on.

John Eliot's first big job after he had learned the Indian language was in a small Indian settlement near the falls of the Charles River. A friendly group of Indians lived there. They seemed interested in listening to his message. To this group John Eliot preached the first sermon in the Indian language. It lasted for one hour and 15 minutes. John Eliot took the verse "Prophesy unto the wind" (Ezek. 37:9) for his text. This was a very appropriate verse because this Indian group's name was "Waban," which meant "the wind."

Even the children were quiet as John Eliot talked of the Lord. After his sermon was finished, he prayed to God in English. But this time he did it because he did not feel that he could really pray in the Indian language. When the service was over, many of the Indians stopped to ask questions. John Eliot answered as many as he could and then promised that he would come back to preach to them.

Some of the Indians wondered why God, who

had all power, did not kill the Devil, who made men bad. Others asked John Eliot if God made the Devil first or man first. They also asked him if all their Indian friends who had died were now in hell since they had not heard the message of the gospel. They asked why God did not give all people good hearts and where little children went when they died. All of these questions gave John Eliot a good chance to talk to them about the Lord Jesus.

They had many other questions, too, such as why sea water was salty and land water was fresh. They wondered why the English people killed the snakes. It was not easy to find answers to all of these questions.

After John Eliot had been preaching for some time, he was able to lead some of the people to the Lord Jesus. Soon the village became known as the Christian village of Nonantum. This meant "rejoicing."

From John Eliot the Indians also received clothing, blankets, spades, axes and other tools. The Indian squaws were given spinning wheels. It was not long before the Indians laid out streets and fenced and planted their fields. They loved John Eliot and tried to obey his teachings, even when he told them that they were not to do any unnecessary work on Sundays. Before long the village of Nanantum became a small trading center. The Indians made brooms, baskets and meal pots. They also sold fish and venison, and when berries were in season, they sold them too.

In spite of the work of John Eliot, it seemed that these "praying Indians," as they were called, were not trusted by most of the white people. John Eliot decided to move up the Charles River to a place called Natick. It was 18 miles away from the reservation. On this place he decided to make a small town. There they would use the laws and rules found in the Bible. He said that his Indians would be "wholly governed by Scripture in all things, both in church and state." The town of Natick was made to take care of about 800 Indians. Almost all of the work was done by the Indians. Streets were made on both sides of the river. Lots were measured, and one lot was given to each family. A round fort was built. A meeting-house was also made. This was used for a school-house during the week and a church on Sunday. While there were some English houses, most of the Indians liked wigwams because they were used to them.

Every two weeks during the summer John Eliot would visit his "praying Indians" at Natick. In order to gather the people together, someone would beat two drums. Everybody knew that this meant they were to go to the meetinghouse. When they got there, John Eliot would preach a sermon in the Indian language, the language he had finally learned and the one the Indians could understand. By this time most of the Indians thought of him as a father. They knew that he was a wonderful man. They were happy to do what he told them to do and thought of him as a real friend.

Everyone else had thought of the Indians as heathen and savage, but John Eliot had been able to help them until they learned to hoe, reap, cut wood, make hay and build stone fences. People would come to visit the village of Natick after they heard what the Indians were doing, just to see whether or not it was true.

John Eliot had clothing, food and farm implements which he would give to the Indians as gifts for sitting and listening to a gospel message. He always brought presents for the children, and an Indian was never turned away empty-handed from his home.

John Eliot gave away much money this way, but at the same time money for this missionary work came from England, from wealthy people who knew what he was doing and believed in his work. In 1649 a corporation in London called "The Society for Promoting and Propagating the Gospel of Jesus Christ in New England," was organized. Through this group John Eliot received much of his support.

Some people wondered if the Indians really accepted Christ as their Saviour or if they just did it in order to get the free gifts, but John Eliot believed that the Indians really loved the Lord Jesus.

John Eliot's biggest ambition was to translate the Bible into the Indian language. From the very first days of his work, he had tried to translate some of the Bible. He knew that if the Indians did accept Christ as their Saviour, they would need God's Word to read, in order to grow and become strong Christians. For ten years he worked on this job. In some cases his translator, Job Nesutan, did not know of an Indian word to match the English King James Version, and when they asked other Indians, some of them would purposely give John Eliot the wrong word to trick him. When his Bible was finally finished, The Society for Promoting and Propagating the Gospel of Jesus Christ in New England helped to pay for the printing.

In spite of all this other work, he kept up his Roxbury congregation and also the education of his own people. One of his prayers was, "Lord, for schools everywhere among us." He founded the Indian College at Cambridge. He also established the Free School in Roxbury, Massachusetts. He made teachers and ministers of many of the Indians who accepted Christ as Saviour, and he regularly wrote reports of his work which were later published as tracts.

When John Eliot first began translating the Bible into the Indian language, he did not know if it ever would be printed, but he continued his work, trusting the Lord and hoping that the London Society would print it. In 1659 John Eliot completed his work, and the London Society began to print it. Four years later, 1500 copies were finished and in use by the Indians. This was the first Bible ever to be printed in America. After this John Eliot wrote an Indian primer, an Indian grammar and an Indian Psalter. By 1674 there were two established Indian churches, 14 Indian towns and 1100 "praying Indians."

John Eliot was faithful to the Lord in telling the Indians about Jesus, and many were saved as a result.

Philip Bliss

Philip Bliss is best known as a song leader, a hymnwriter and an evangelist. Another thing which made Philip Bliss famous was the fact that he became the song leader for such outstanding men as D. L. Moody, D. W. Whittle and others.

Philip Bliss—Singing Evangelist

If you have ever sat in church looking at the names of hymnwriters in your hymnbook, you have no doubt seen the name of P. P. Bliss.

Philip Paul Bliss had a very fine Christian father and a lovely Christian mother. Philip was born in the state of Pennsylvania on July 9, 1838. His home was like a log cabin rather than a home like yours.

Philip's father always had a family prayer time when he gathered his family together to read the Bible and to pray.

Until Philip Bliss was ten years old, he was not able to go to a regular school. His mother was his teacher. She not only taught him school subjects but also, and especially, the Bible. His father taught him to love music and to sing.

When Philip Bliss was 11 years old, he left home to get a job. He was big for his age, so he soon found work on a farm. Two years later he found other work which paid him more money. He was to help the cook in a lumber camp. The wages for this work were nine dollars a month. After doing this work the very best he knew how, he was given a promotion and became a log cutter. He only worked at this job for one year and then was given another promotion. This time it was as a sawmill worker in the sawmill.

Even after Philip Bliss had received these promotions, he was not satisfied. He did not want to stay as a regular worker. He wanted to make something better of himself so that he could get a very good job. Every time he had a chance, he would go to school. Even though he was not sure what kind of work he wanted, he felt that he should keep studying in order to learn all he could.

Philip was a Christian, so while he worked in the lumber camp, he tried to be a testimony and live a good Christian life before the men in the camp. This was not always easy, because often the men, who were rough and tough, would make fun of him.

By the time Philip was 17 years old, he had decided he wanted to teach school. But first he had to finish his own education. So he went to college to finish his studies. Now he was ready to teach. His first teaching job was in New York.

Since the people there only had school in the winter, Philip Bliss had to go back to the farm during the summer months.

Mr. J. G. Towner (another name which you have seen in your church hymnbook) became a very good friend to Philip Bliss. In fact, it was Mr. Towner who gave Philip Bliss his first singing lessons. The only other help he had ever received was from his father. When Mr. Towner heard Philip Bliss sing, he realized that he had a very fine voice and helped him to make it even better.

One day Mr. Towner helped Philip go to a music convention in another part of Pennsylvania. While there, Philip Bliss met a man by the name of W. B. Bradbury. Mr. Bradbury was a well-known writer of children's songs. (If you look in your hymnbook, you will find that he wrote one of your favorite Sunday school songs, "Jesus Loves Me.")

It was after meeting these outstanding men of music that Philip Bliss decided he would continue his musical training.

On June 1, 1859, Philip Bliss married a very fine Christian young lady. Philip decided to work on the farm which belonged to his wife's father, in order to continue his study in music and still support the family. As he learned more and more about music, he also began to teach to earn more money.

For three summers Philip Bliss went to the Academy of Music in New York. He studied very hard while there and worked as hard during the rest of the year at home.

In a short time the people of his hometown recognized that Philip Bliss was a good musician. He learned to compose songs. Almost all of the songs which he wrote at this time were secular songs; that is, they were not especially Christian. He was paid good money for his work, and Philip

17

thought it would be wonderful to have this kind of job.

A short time later he and his wife moved to Chicago, where Philip worked for a music house. He held music conventions in different places and also did a great deal of concert work. Philip Bliss was becoming very popular by this time, and much of his music was being printed in books.

One night Philip Bliss walked by a church in Chicago. There he noticed that D. L. Moody was holding meetings. Philip decided to go in and listen to the well-known evangelist.

As a rule, Mr. Moody had a song leader with him, but on this particular night the song leader was not there. Philip Bliss was in the audience, and he sang quite loud and helped to make the song service much better. Mr. Moody heard him; after the service, the evangelist stopped to talk with him. He asked Mr. Bliss to come and help him with his meetings whenever they were both in Chicago. Philip promised and from then on helped in the Moody meetings whenever it was possible.

Another evangelist, D. W. Whittle, also met Philip Bliss and asked him to help in his services. It was Mr. Whittle who later made it possible for Mr. Bliss and his family to move into his own vacant apartment. He also helped Philip Bliss to become the choir director in a large church in Chicago.

While the Bliss family was living in Mr. Whittle's house and while he was working with this choir, Philip Bliss wrote two of his best-known songs. I am sure you have sung at least one of them. The songs are "Hold the Fort" and "Jesus Loves Even Me."

There are a number of other songs for which this man wrote the words, the music, or both. Some of the best known are: "Let the Lower Lights Be Burning," "Almost Persuaded," "Hallelujah! What a Saviour!" "I Will Sing of My Redeemer," "Dare to Be a Daniel," "It Is Well with My Soul," "The Light of the World Is Jesus," "Whosoever Will" and many, many more.

All during the time that Philip Bliss was writing these gospel songs, leading the church choir and helping in special meetings, he was still working for the music house in Chicago. One day he received a letter from Evangelist D. L. Moody, who was holding special meetings in Scotland. Mr. Moody told Philip Bliss that he ought to think about giving up his job in order to become a singing evangelist. He told Mr. Bliss that he could sing the gospel, just as evangelists preached the gospel. At first Philip Bliss was not sure this was the right thing for him to do. He talked it over with his wife, and together they prayed and asked the Lord to show them His will.

A short time later Mr. Bliss went to Waukegan, Illinois, to help his friend, Mr. Whittle, in some services there. At first the meetings did not seem to go too well, and Philip Bliss thought it was God's way of showing him that he should not go into evangelistic work. On the very last night of meetings, Mr. Bliss sang his own song, "Almost Persuaded." During the singing of this invitation song, people began to walk down the church aisle to the front for prayer. Many sinners were saved that night, and scores of Christians were blessed as they heard Mr. Bliss sing. After this meeting Philip Bliss knew for sure that God was calling him to be a singing evangelist.

The next afternoon Mr. Bliss made a promise to God to give up his secular songwriting, his music conventions and even his work at the music house, in order to give all his time to God's work.

This was not an easy decision to make because it would mean that no money would be coming in regularly to support his family unless the Lord sent it in. But Philip Bliss knew that the same God who had called him to be a singing evangelist would also take care of the needs of his family.

From that day on, Philip Bliss helped in evangelistic meetings. He worked with well-known men such as D. W. Whittle and D. L. Moody. He traveled a great deal, going from state to state, singing about the Lord Jesus. Philip Bliss did some preaching as well as singing and especially enjoyed working with the young people.

On Christmas, 1876, Philip Bliss went home to be with his family in Pennsylvania. He had promised D. L. Moody that he would be back in Chicago in early January to help in some meetings. But while Mr. Bliss was in Pennsylvania for the Christmas holidays, Mr. Moody sent him a telegram asking the singer to be in Chicago on the Sunday after Christmas. Philip Bliss wired back that he would be there, but he never reached Chicago, for on Friday, December 29, 1876, Mr. and Mrs. Philip Bliss were in a terrible train wreck in Ohio which took their lives.

How people missed the singing evangelist! Two days after the terrible accident D. L. Moody held a memorial service for the singer. More than 8000 people attended this meeting, and about 4000 more stood outside of the building because they were not able to get in.

One of the greatest songwriters, singers and Christians of that day had finished his work. He would not preach another sermon, direct another choir, sing another song or write another hymn. But what he had done for the Lord would help people to come to Christ from that day on.

George Washington Carver

George Washington Carver is best known as a scientist who loved Christ Jesus as his Saviour. He was black and not accepted by most of the people, but he became a very famous scientist. He developed many new ideas for food, medicine and other things. George Washington Carver is also known as a former slave boy.

George Washington Carver—Slave Boy and Scientist

He was just a black child, born near Diamond Grove, Missouri, during the early days of the Civil War, probably 1864. He was the baby of a slave mother. She fought, first, for the life of her baby and, then, for her own life.

While the country was at war, some robbers came and took the child and his mother away. In their hurry to get away, they separated the child and his mother. Nothing was ever heard of the slave woman again.

Moses Carver, the owner of the slave woman, gave the robbers a $300 racehorse in order to get the child back. Mrs. Carver named him George Washington Carver. All through his young life little

23

George was sickly and weak. And later, as he grew, he was unable to do heavy work.

Even though George loved his white masters very much, he still thought about his slave mother. He had not seen her since he was a small child. He wondered where she was and what she was doing. He often thought of the little hut that had been their home.

When George Washington Carver was ten years old, he became very interested in nature. He spent many hours in the fields, carefully examining every blade of grass and blossom from the flowers. Many times he would find some paper and make drawings of these plants. Soon he changed from drawing them to painting them. George loved nature and he loved the God of nature too.

Because he was black, George was often shunned by people. This made him spend more time talking with the Lord Jesus. He knew that Jesus did not care if his skin was black. He learned to spend much time in prayer. He talked to God about all the things he did and wanted to do. When George was an old man, he told people that God had made him a good scientist. While it is true that George Washington Carver was a genius, it was God who helped him in everything he did.

At first George was not able to go to a school, but he made good use of a speller that had been given to him. He would lie flat on his stomach on the rough, hard floor and study from his spelling book every day. At first he found it very hard to learn. But George had made up his mind that he was going to learn to read and write, so he worked hard at his studies.

After some time George Washington Carver found that he could go to school. The school was far from the Carver house, and he had no money, but how he wanted to attend! The law did not say that he had to go, as it does now, nor did his parents force him to go. He went because he wanted to go. The log benches were hard and many of the students were not friendly. But George had come to study, and these other things did not matter to him. Whenever George saw a boy who did not seem to have friends, he made that boy his own special friend. He tried to be kind and good to everyone.

The first night George was away from the Carver plantation, he slept in a horse stable. He did not have any food, so he had to earn money to buy it. For this he went from house to house doing odd jobs. After walking from one house to another looking for work, he was finally hired by a family to be their houseboy.

George was very happy to get this work. The people liked George too. He worked hard and never complained about the long hours. Because of his job he did not have time to play like other boys. He would get up very early to do as many chores as he had time for. Then he would go to his studies at school. After school hours he would again begin his work—washing dishes, scrubbing the floor, milking the cows and feeding the pigs.

Almost everyone in the school made fun of George, not only because he found it hard to read sentences and learn big words, but also because he was the only black child in the school. His white classmates said that a slave did not need an education. Not long after that, however, these same

25

classmates noticed that even though George was only 11 years old, he was the smartest student in the school. George had studied so hard that he was "smarter" than the teacher.

When George Washington Carver was 17 years old, he went back to visit the Carver plantation. How proud Mr. and Mrs. Carver were as they listened to their boy! They remembered how they had once ransomed him for the price of a horse.

George had been gone from the Carver home for seven years studying at school, but he was still a lover of nature. Early in the morning, the first day back on the plantation, George crept out into the morning air to look over the plants and bushes. He studied each flower.

He made his way back to the little hut that had once been the home of his own slave mother. It was nearly tumbled down, but it was still sacred to George. It had been their home. He walked into the almost empty room. There in the corner was the old bunk bed. On the other side of the room stood a broken chair and an old wooden stand. Everything else had been taken away. George wiped away the tears which fell from his eyes, walked away and never went back to the little hut again.

When summer was over, George thought of school. He began to think of a place where he could get more education. He had finished his regular high school education. Now he wanted to go on and study more about nature and especially flowers. He tried many different schools, but he was always turned down because he was black. Finally he was accepted at Iowa State College, and before long he earned his Bachelor of Science degree. He was an assistant botanist and was in charge of the greenhouses at this same college while he worked on his master's degree.

After some time, however, one of his assistants told the school board that he thought a Negro should not be in such a high position. So George Washington Carver lost his job. In spite of this, George Carver knew that things did not "just happen." They were always sent from God. Soon he realized that he had more time to do research work. He would help the farmers find out why their cattle were dying. He would work with food and with flowers.

One of Mr. Carver's greatest discoveries was the peanut. From this he produced such things as lard, vinegar, relishes, printer's ink, dyes, plastic, soaps, coffee, soft drinks, wood stains and many other things.

While other scientists looked into the microscope only to find that their work had been in vain, George Washington Carver, the black scientist, spent much time in prayer. His faith and his prayer, rather than his microscope, made him such a success. For each problem and each discovery, Mr. Carver spent much time praying to the Lord and waiting on Him for results.

This man who loved God so much turned many weeds into food and made waste places into gardens. His help to people has never been forgotten.

Friends and other great men of the world came to visit George Washington Carver in his small laboratory. Whenever they came, Mr. Carver would explain to them the Scriptures and give his own testimony of his love for the Lord. George Carver especially liked to read about the Lord Jesus and His parables. His well-worn Bible proved to everyone that he spent much time reading God's Word.

George Washington Carver died on January 5, 1943. His last words were: "They are preparing for me, in the other world."

Although this black slave boy never went to the mission field and never pastored a church, the Lord used him and his testimony in witnessing of the Lord Jesus Christ to many hundreds of people.

God needs Christian workers, scientists and doctors today. He calls Christian people to be good in their work and to tell others about Christ. One of the poems that George Washington Carver wrote makes an excellent motto:

You're well equipped for what you choose;
You have arms and legs and a brain to use.

Charles Finney

Charles Finney is best known because he became a great evangelist. Even though he began to study to be a lawyer and although he never went to a Bible school or college for ministers, God used him as one of the greatest evangelists of his day. It was through Charles Finney that many revivals began.

Charles Finney—Great Evangelist

Charles Grandison Finney was born in Warren, Connecticut, August 29, 1792. His father was Sylvester Finney, a farmer. This was during the time that George Washington was the President of the United States and there were only 15 states in the Union.

Charles did not come from a Christian family. In fact, it was not until after Charles Finney had accepted Christ as his Saviour that he prayed or heard prayer in his home. His father had never prayed as far as Charles could remember.

Charles Finney never read the Bible as a young boy, but when he was 29 years old and a law student in college, he bought one and read it.

Charles's father was more interested in novels than in the Bible. In fact, he named Charles after one of the characters in a novel which he read, Charles Grandison.

When Charles was two years old, his parents moved from Connecticut to New York. This did not help as far as his Christian training was concerned. Charles still did not hear the gospel of the Lord Jesus.

He went to school regularly and learned the things which seemed necessary to learn in those days. At the age of 16 Charles was considered an educated boy, so he quit school in order to teach.

Even then, the only time he heard a gospel message was when he was traveling somewhere or when a traveling preacher came to his community.

One day a "meetinghouse" was built near the Finney farm. A pastor came to live in that area, but just about that time the Finney family moved again.

Then Charles's interest seemed to shift toward music. Charles Finney met people who seemed to be very fine musicians. They helped to give him a real interest in music. He learned to read music, to sing, to play the violin and the cello. He studied hard at his music. Since he especially enjoyed the cello, he decided to specialize in it.

After he had taught school for awhile, he saved enough money to buy his instrument. He studied harmony and composition and soon became an outstanding musician.

At the age of 20 Charles went back to visit his home in Warren, Connecticut, where he had been born. There was a college there now, so Charles planned to attend the Warren Academy and other schools in the area. At this time he decided he would become a lawyer. Receiving some books from a lawyer friend, he began to study very diligently. Hour after hour, night after night, Charles Finney studied his law books. After two years of hard study, he was able to set up a law practice, and his business began to grow. But Charles Finney did not seem to be interested in church.

One day the Rev. George Gale, pastor of the Presbyterian Church, came to visit Mr. Finney in his law office. He invited him to attend church and even lead the choir. Charles Finney took an interest in the things the minister said, especially since he was interested in music.

While studying his law books, Charles noticed that they often referred to many of the laws of the Bible. This made him so curious that he finally went out and bought a Bible. It seemed that the more he read the Bible, and the more he attended church, the more he wanted to read the Bible. Through both the reading of the Bible and attending church, Charles Finney learned that he was not ready to go to heaven if he should die. He talked often with the pastor and listened as he preached from God's Book each week. After all this, he wondered if the things he was hearing about the gospel and the Christian religion were for him. He had not had any spiritual training in his home, so it was hard for him to believe these new things about God.

For two years Charles Finney studied his Bible every chance he had. He began to attend prayer meetings at the church. More and more he realized that he was a sinner.

One night as he was thinking about it seriously, he got down on his knees and prayed to God. He said, "I promise that I am going to give my heart to Thee." Charles was sincere in that promise, but somehow he kept putting off his decision.

As he continued to read his Bible, he found that his heart was proud. He realized that he was afraid someone would see him reading his Bible and praying. Whenever Charles prayed in his room, he would put paper in the keyhole to be sure that no one could hear him. If someone knocked at his door while he was reading, he would quickly cover his Bible with his law books, for he did not want them to see him studying God's Word. For two or three days Charles Finney was very concerned about his soul. He was afraid that he might die, and he knew that if he died he would not go to heaven.

One day as he was walking to his office, he thought he heard a voice speaking to him. "What are you waiting for? Didn't you promise to give your heart to God? Are you trying to work your way to God?"

Charles Finney stopped to think over the words. It was then that he realized what he was doing. He was trying to work his way to heaven, when all along the Lord Jesus had given His life on Calvary for the salvation of Charles Finney.

Instead of going to his office that day, he turned and went to the woods. He had gone there many times for walks, but this time he was going to pray. He wanted to be away from everyone, except God. Even here, Charles Finney found it hard to pray. Every time he heard the leaves rustle, he thought someone was coming, so he would quickly open his eyes and stop praying. All at once he realized that he thought more of people seeing him than of being with a holy God who could forgive his sins. Suddenly he thought of a Scripture verse that he had read. "Then shall ye call upon me, and ye shall go and pray unto me, and I will hearken unto you. And ye shall seek me, and find me, when ye shall search for me with all your heart" (Jer. 29:12,13). Charles Finney again dropped to his knees and prayed, "Lord, I take Thee at Thy word."

God's Word said that when a sinner searched with all his heart, God would hear him, and certainly Charles Finney was searching with all his heart. All at once a very peaceful feeling came over him. He knew that God had forgiven his sins.

As he walked from the woods and back into the city, he looked to see what time it was. It was noon! He thought he had only prayed for a short time, but he had been in the woods all morning. As he came to his law office, he found that his partner had gone home for dinner. Charles Finney was alone—alone with God.

He took down his favorite instrument, the cello, and began to play and sing some of the gospel songs he knew. All at once he began to weep. He tried to stop the tears, but he could not. He had met God that day, and his whole life had been changed.

The next morning Charles Finney went to his office. When his partner came in, Charles talked to him about what had happened in his own life and what Christ could do for him. His partner was so surprised that he walked out of the room, leaving Mr. Finney alone. But two or three days later he, too, accepted Charles Finney's Saviour as his own.

33

One day as Charles Finney was thinking about his conversion, he remembered that he had made a promise many months before. He had said to the Lord, "If I am ever saved, I will preach the gospel." For two years he had been a good lawyer, but suddenly it seemed that his interest in law was gone. God was showing him that he should become an evangelist.

As Mr. Finney began to speak to different people about the Lord Jesus, many of them were converted. The people in the neighborhood noticed the change in Charles Finney's life. Even the work at the church, with Rev. George Gale, seemed to grow.

Some time after Charles Finney had accepted the Lord Jesus as his Saviour, he decided to visit his father and talk with him about accepting Christ as Saviour. Charles talked not only with his father but also with his mother and brother. In just a few days he had led all of them to the Lord.

Charles stayed in his hometown for a few days. While he was there, he talked to many of the people about their souls. God used his testimony, and soon a revival started in the church community. Many of the people were saved.

Some of Charles Finney's friends decided that he was a man God would use, so they wanted to send him to a minister's school. Charles refused this and asked his pastor to help him to learn the Scriptures.

While Charles Finney had been a lawyer, he had learned many things. One of the most important things came from a Supreme Court judge who said, "Charlie, you win a legal case by telling it

34

simply; never read it. Repeat it many times, but tell it simply."

Since Mr. Finney knew this was the way to move a jury and win a case, he decided that this must also be the way to move people's hearts, so he never wrote down any of his sermons. Then after he had preached his sermon, he would write it down in outline form so he would know what had been said. He always knew in his heart what he wanted to say, and he told it very simply and directly.

Charles Finney was 32 years old when he married a fine Christian young lady, Miss Lydia Andrews.

One day as Charles Finney was preaching in a small village, he tried to explain to the people why they needed to become Christians. At the end of the service he gave an invitation, asking people to stand if they would believe on the Lord Jesus Christ and be saved. Suddenly, he changed his mind and turned his invitation around and asked only those who refused to accept Christ to remain seated. He asked all the others to stand. The people looked angrily at each other, but they did not move. Charles Finney realized that these people were lost, so he said, "You have taken your stand; you have rejected Christ and His gospel."

The people became so angry that they got up and walked out of the door. As Mr. Finney watched them leave, he said, "I am sorry for you. I will preach to you once more, the Lord willing— tomorrow night." All the people left except one old deacon. After everyone else was out of the building, the deacon said, "Brother Finney, I believe that you have done the very thing that

needed to be done and that we shall see results."
Mr. Finney and the deacon decided they would
spend the entire next day in prayer, each in his
own house in the morning and together in the
afternoon.

The people had been so angry when they left
that Mr. Finney did not know if they would return
to the service that night or not. Early in the evening, as Charles Finney and the deacon left the
woods where they had been praying, they went to
the church and found that the building was
packed.

That night there was no singing in the meeting
and no announcements. Charles Finney stood to
preach his sermon right away. He could see all
during the service that God was speaking to hearts
and that people were under conviction. Rather
than give an invitation, he dismissed the congregation.

All during the night, people tried to get in
touch with Mr. Finney to ask him to pray for
them. The revival had started. People were being
saved, and God was blessing the ministry of Charles
Finney.

In another community not far from where Mr.
Finney had preached before, the same thing
happened. As he brought the message from God's
Word, the entire church, in fact, almost the whole
community, was converted.

After holding meetings in many communities
in New York, Charles Finney had the reputation of
being a great evangelist. One morning as he went to
visit a mill, he stopped and talked to a young lady
who was working there. In a few seconds she broke
out in tears, confessing her sins to the Lord. Then

one worker after another came to Mr. Finney asking him how to be saved. When the owner of the mill saw what was going on, he said, "Stop the mill. It is more important that our souls should be saved than that this factory run." All the machines stopped, and all of the workers went to a room to hear Mr. Finney preach. In just a few days almost every worker in the mill had come to the Lord Jesus for salvation.

Mr. Finney then had the chance to preach to some of the lumbermen who were working in that area. Many of them accepted Christ as their Saviour and went back to their families and told what Christ had done for them. There were no schools or churches here, but the lumbermen witnessed to others in the area.

Two years later, when Charles Finney conducted meetings nearby, some of the lumbermen came to ask him if there were any way they could get a minister to come and preach to them. They told the evangelist that about 5000 people had been converted since he visited the lumber camp. God had used the testimonies of these men to start a revival in their own community, even though there was not one minister anywhere nearby.

It seemed that every place Charles Finney went, God brought about a real revival. Mr. Finney preached simply and carefully, as he had learned to speak through his law practice, and the Holy Spirit convicted men and women of their sin.

On a Sunday evening in 1875, near his 83d birthday, his work ended. Outside the church, he heard the choir singing and even tried to sing with them just a little. Then he suffered a heart attack and went to be with the Lord Jesus, his Saviour.

God had used Charles Finney in a very special way to start revivals throughout the country. Hundreds and hundreds of people were saved because Charles Finney, the great evangelist, was faithful in doing what he had promised: "If I am ever saved, I will preach the gospel."

David Livingstone

David Livingstone is best known because he was an explorer, as well as a missionary. After he went to Africa, he went to the inner part of that country to explore the land, to find the people and to teach them about God. Another thing which made David Livingstone famous was when the world thought he was lost and sent men to find him.

David Livingstone—Explorer for God

David Livingstone was born in Blantyre, Scotland, on March 19, 1813, and came from a poor family. There were four other children—two sisters and two brothers. Mr. and Mrs. Livingstone taught their children many things, but one of the most important lessons was the one of honesty. "Always be honest," his father would say, "no matter what it costs."

At the age of ten, David Livingstone began working in a cotton factory. His hours were long; he started work every morning at six and worked until eight at night. After that he went to classes until ten at night and then went home to study for another two hours. It was almost always midnight before he went to bed and often much later. Sometimes his mother would find him in bed reading a book until the wee hours of the morning. He loved to read and got books on various subjects.

When David was 16 years old, he read the story of Gutzlaff, the missionary to China. Through the reading of this book David decided that he, too, wanted to go to China and tell the people about the Lord Jesus.

After nine years of hard work in the cotton factory, David was given a promotion with good pay. Through this increase in pay, David Livingstone was later able to go to medical school.

He tried hard to keep his mind on his work, but this was not easy because he had something else on his mind. He liked the subject of geography and read it as often as he had a chance. As he read about the different countries, he would imagine himself in these places, exploring unknown parts where God would have him go.

It was while thinking about these things that David Livingstone met the great missionary adventurer Robert Moffat. While talking to Dr. Moffat, David was shown an unexplored territory on the map. The great explorer said, "There has never been a missionary there. That is your field." At that time David Livingstone committed himself to the Lord for the dark continent of Africa.

Immediately he began to study. He studied medicine, for every missionary was expected to heal the sick as well as to preach the gospel. Then he studied different languages because he felt that he was a soldier preparing for war on the great African battlefield. After much preparation, he

40

finally was ready to sail. It was a long, tiresome voyage, but David spent much of his time telling the people on the ship about the Lord. Every Sunday he would preach to the sailors and tell them of the love of the Lord Jesus Christ.

After traveling for three months, David Livingstone finally reached his destination. Africa—at last! When he reached the shores of the dark continent, he did not stay there. Instead, he traveled 700 miles inland by ox wagon into the very heart of Africa. The oxen traveled very slowly, and this part of the trip took two more months.

David Livingstone had expected to see Dr. and Mrs. Moffat when he arrived, but as yet they had not left England. So David decided to learn the language. He first gained the confidence of the natives. Through his hard work, his friendliness and his ability to help them with medicine when they were sick, he soon was able to speak their language. During his stay the missionary knew that this was not the place God wanted him. He felt that he should go farther inland to the places where the people had never heard about Jesus.

David Livingstone traveled many miles to preach in the villages. One time he took a trip of 100 miles to visit the chief of a certain tribe. As he preached the message of the love of God for all people, the chief of the village asked, "If it is true that all men who die unforgiven are lost forever, why did not your people come to tell us this story before now?" Mr. Livingstone knew that action, not words, was important now. Only a short time later the chief's daughter became very sick. David Livingstone took care of her and gave her medicine which soon made her well and strong again. This made the chief happy. He listened to all that Mr. Livingstone had to say about Jesus and soon accepted Him as his Saviour. This opened the way for David Livingstone to preach the gospel to the whole tribe.

While working in the interior of Africa, David Livingstone helped many people by showing them how to dig trenches, work in their fields and care for their physical needs. He gave medicine to many sick people, and some of the people walked more than a hundred miles just to be treated by David Livingstone.

One of the big problems in this section of the jungle was the lions. They often killed the cattle owned by the natives. Sometimes they even killed the people themselves. Mr. Livingstone felt that something had to be done. He knew that if one pride, or group, of lions could be killed, all the rest would leave that area.

One day while he and some of his native helpers were walking through the jungle, they came upon a lion. Carefully aiming his gun, Mr. Livingstone shot at it. Thinking he had killed the beast, he continued on his way. But in just a few seconds, the angry, wounded lion suddenly leaped at David Livingstone. The natives who were with him knew that this would be the end of their missionary friend, and they screamed at the top of their voices. The lion heard the screams and suddenly turned to look. Then he decided to run after them rather than after David Livingstone. This gave the missionary enough time to aim again. This time he killed the lion. The Lord had been with him and had protected him.

After David Livingstone had been in Africa for two years, he began to push farther inland. Already he had gone farther into the jungle than any white man, but he was not satisfied. He wanted to reach unknown and untouched tribes and tell them of the love of Christ. While talking to some of these inland people, David Livingstone heard of the "smoke that sounds." Since David was an explorer at heart, he wanted to find out what this was. He continued to work his way inland for ten days, and finally he heard a great, roaring sound. Then he saw what was called "smoke that sounds." David Livingstone, God's explorer, had discovered one of the greatest natural wonders of the world—the roaring, foaming Victoria Falls.

Every day David Livingstone realized that there was more work to be done in helping to spread the gospel to those natives who were even farther inland than he had gone. He wanted to go there and tell them, as he had told the others, of the Lord Jesus.

One day in 1869 the report came back to America that David Livingstone, the great missionary-explorer, had gone so deeply into the jungles that he was lost. Nothing had been heard of him, and he was thought to be dead. At this time James Gorden Bennett, the editor of the *New York Herald*, called a young reporter into his office. He told him that he was going to send him to Africa to find David Livingstone. The young reporter, Henry Stanley, left the American shores for what was then called "the dark continent." After much searching, Mr. Stanley finally found the missionary in the depths of the jungles, sick with a native fever. Mr. Stanley gave the missionary food and medicine, and quickly David Livingstone was restored to health. Together, the missionary and the reporter explored more of the African interior.

David Livingstone continued his work for Christ. Early in the morning of May 1, 1873, David Livingstone was called home to be with the Lord. He had given 37 years of his life to reach the unsaved peoples of Africa. One of Mr. Livingstone's last statements was "Nothing earthly will make me give up my work in despair. I encourage myself in the Lord, my God, and go forward."

Mr. Livingstone's men were faithful to their master. After his death, they did not leave him. Carefully they carried him to a hut, away from the villagers who were superstitious about death. They opened his body, took out his heart and buried it in the country Mr. Livingstone loved so well. His body is buried in London's Westminster Abbey.

George Mueller

George Mueller is best known because of his faith in God. He believed God for everything—food, housing, people and help. While he took care of hundreds of orphan children and while often there was little or no food on hand, George Mueller knew that God would never fail him and that He would provide. And he was right. George Mueller's life of prayer and the fact that he depended completely on God made him famous.

George Mueller—Father to the Fatherless

George Mueller was born September 27, 1805, in Prussia, part of Germany. His father was a government worker who collected taxes from business companies. George received a good education but did not learn to use money right. He and his brother were given money very freely with the hope that they would learn to use it, but they spent it carelessly. When asked what happened to this money, George lied about it. Very often he stole money from different places and lied about where he got it. Soon one lie had led to another, and George fell deeper and deeper into sin.

Before George Mueller had reached the age of ten, he had become an expert thief, cheater and liar. By the time he was 14, he was spending much time playing cards and drinking. George was even drunk the night his mother died.

George Mueller went to confirmation class just as many boys did, but he did not seem to pay attention to the lessons from the Bible. When he was to be confirmed on Easter, he even took some of the money that was to go to the minister. George did all these things because he did not know Christ as his Saviour. He did not really want to be a thief and a cheater, but sin made him do these things.

When George Mueller was 16, he was put in jail for running up a big hotel bill and leaving without paying it.

George's father heard about what had happened, so he went and paid the hotel bill and other bills and had his son released. After this, George seemed to improve a little, but there was sin in his heart and life.

Soon George Mueller began to study and read. He owned about 300 books, but a Bible was not among them. Even though George went to a school to prepare to be a minister, he was not living for the Lord Jesus.

At this school George met a friend. His name was Beta. In no time at all George and Beta began to do all kinds of sinful things. One day they stole some money and took a long trip. After they got back Beta realized he had not been living for Jesus and confessed his sin to God.

George and Beta went to a little prayer meeting together one day. Here some of the men met each

46

week to sing, read the Scriptures and kneel for prayer. It was here that George Mueller saw what a terrible life he had been living. He kept going to those meetings, and soon he gave his life to the Lord Jesus.

After George Mueller gave his whole life to the Lord, he wrote to his father to tell him that he had been saved from all his sin and asked his father to take Christ as his Saviour, too, but his father became angry.

Up to this point George had been getting money from his father, but when he learned that his father was angry, he felt it would be better not to accept more money from him.

In 1830, after he had lived a few months in England, Mr. Mueller accepted a call from the people of the Ebenezer Chapel in Tiegnmouth to be their pastor. This church had only 18 members, and they decided to pay their minister $275 a year. This money came in because the people used to rent the pews, or seats, in the church. Mr. Mueller did not like this idea. He soon announced to his congregation that he no longer wanted to receive a regular salary but that a box would be placed at the door of the chapel, and anyone wanting to help in his support could leave his offering there.

From that day on, George Mueller began to live by faith and soon became known as "the man of faith." During this same year he married Miss Mary Groves. She was a real help to him in his work for God. She, too, loved the Lord and wanted to do all that God had for them to do.

At the end of the first year of his work at the Ebenezer Chapel, Mr. Mueller had received about

$660 through gifts of his friends. If he had stayed on the salary, he would have received $275.

George Mueller read a great deal. In fact, he read his Bible through about two hundred times. One day while reading his Bible, he found in Psalm 68:5 the words "a father of the fatherless." As he read, he said, "God is their Father and, therefore, has promised to provide for them, and I have only to remind Him of the need of these poor children and have it supplied."

George Mueller then decided to rent a house and open an orphanage to care for children.

On the opening day not one child had come. It was then that Mr. Mueller realized that he had asked the Lord to supply every need for the institution, but he had not asked the Lord to send in the orphans. Again George Mueller prayed, and the very next day the first application was received. One month later there were 26 orphans in the home.

Seven months after opening the first orphan's home, a second home was opened, and 30 children were admitted there. One year later a home for boys was opened. Now Mr. and Mrs. Mueller were in charge of the three orphan homes with a total of 96 orphans. Not once during this year did God fail to supply a single meal, and not once during Mr. Mueller's life was a meal more than 30 minutes late.

Because the neighbors complained about too much noise from the children and because Mr. Mueller felt that the rented homes were not big enough and the playgrounds were too small, he set out to have a new building made. This one would have plenty of room for garden space where the

48

children could be trained and vegetables grown to use in feeding all the orphans. A Christian architect offered his services free of charge, and the work was soon done. Two hundred seventy-five children then moved into this new home.

Before the work of George Mueller was done, five large orphanages had been erected. All the money for these buildings and all the expenses of keeping the work going for the 35 years had come in because George Mueller, his wife, the orphans and many other people had prayed, and God answered their prayers.

Mr. Mueller's wife died February 6, 1870. She had been a real helper for almost 40 years. She died just one month after the last of the new orphan homes was completed. Mr. Mueller preached the funeral service, using the verse from Psalm 119:68: "Thou art good, and doest good."

Sixteen months after Mrs. Mueller died, their only daughter, Lydia Mueller, was married to James Wright. He had been working with Mr. and Mrs. Mueller in their work at the orphanage. It was through Mr. Wright that George Mueller felt he would be able to leave the work of the orphanage for a time in order to travel and do missionary work. Mr. Mueller was 70 years old when he left England for his first missionary tour. For 17 years he traveled in missionary work.

On Mr. Mueller's 90th birthday he preached to the congregation where he had been the pastor for 69 years. His last sermon, preached on the Sunday evening before his death, was on the verse: "For we know that if our earthly house of this tabernacle were dissolved, we have a building of God, an house not made with hands, eternal in the heavens" (II Cor. 5:1). Such a message must have been chosen by the Holy Spirit to close Mr. Mueller's life. He died during that night.

Through the years people have wondered about such great faith as that of George Mueller. The secret of this faith was in his close contact with the Lord. Mr. Mueller spent much time in reading the Bible and in prayer.

George Mueller had been the father to more than 10,000 orphans, and God blessed both his life and their lives.

Dwight L. Moody

D. L. Moody is best known as one of the world's most famous evangelists. He began as a Sunday school worker, bringing boys and girls to a building where they could hear about Jesus. Then God led him to be a preacher in the United States and in other countries too.

Dwight L. Moody—God's New Worker

Dwight Lyman Moody was born in Northfield, Massachusetts, in 1837, on his mother's birthday—February 5. Dwight's mother was a fine woman and a real influence on Dwight's life, even after he went into God's service.

When Dwight Moody was just a little more than four years of age, his father died suddenly. It was a real shock to the little boy. He was in school that day and had to be called out of class to be told of his father's death. Mr. Moody left seven children to be cared for. Dwight was child number six. Then, just one month after the death of Dwight's father, Mrs. Moody gave birth to twins. Now there were nine children to provide for.

When Mrs. Moody could not pay the bills that had been left, the bill collectors came and took everything she owned. They even took the firewood. This made things very hard for Mrs. Moody. Her oldest child was only 13 years old, hardly old enough to go out and get a job. It was hard for her to support and take care of nine children. Some of the neighbors told Mrs. Moody that she should let some of the children out for adoption, but Mrs. Moody said she would keep her family together as long as she was able.

Things were very hard for the Moody family. Sometimes they did not have much to eat, but they never starved. God always provided for them. Once when there was a big snowstorm, Mrs. Moody kept all the children in bed until it was exactly time to go to school, for there was no wood for the fire and the house was very cold.

Dwight Moody was a pleasant boy. He was also a boy full of pranks. Although his mother was very godly, Dwight did not seem to be too interested in things of religion. Mrs. Moody read to her family from God's Word and a book of devotions every day. On Sunday she gathered them all together and went to church. Nevertheless, Dwight was bored with church. His mother had tried to teach him to pray, but he said that he had tried it and it "didn't work," so he didn't spend much time in prayer.

Another thing that Mrs. Moody taught her children was that when they made a promise, they had to keep it. She told them that a promise was something that must never be broken. One day Dwight quit a job he had promised to keep. His reason for quitting was that he didn't like the food he got at that place. He said it was always the same. When Mrs. Moody heard what her son had done, she sent him back and made him finish the job, for as she said, "You promised." This lesson was something that Dwight Moody never forgot as long as he lived.

As Dwight grew older, he began to realize how important an education was. He had not been too interested in his schooling up to this time, but now he began to study seriously.

One day Dwight was in the woods cutting logs. His brother Edwin was with him. "I'm tired of this," said Dwight. "I'm not going to stay around here any longer. I'm going someplace to get some other work."

Dwight had two uncles who were in the shoe business in Boston. He decided he would go to see them about getting a job. When he talked to them about a job, they turned him down. But Dwight Moody was not discouraged. He went on to Clinton, Massachusetts. There he found a job in a bookstore. His job was to address wrappers. Somehow, this job did not satisfy him, so he went to Boston again. He talked to his uncles again to see if it would be possible to get a job in their store. Finally, they agreed to take him if he would do certain things. They asked him to live in the house they chose, go to their church and Sunday school and promise not to drink or gamble. Dwight promised, so he was given the job as store boy, doing odds and ends.

It was here that Dwight Moody decided that he would become a successful businessman. His ambition was to make $100,000. Instead of wasting his spare time, he studied the business and the prices of all the goods. Before too long, his uncles noticed how well he was doing his work and made him one of their salesmen.

Being away from home, Dwight got homesick at times, so he wrote to his mother in Northfield quite often.

Since Dwight had promised his uncles that he would attend church and Sunday school, he was faithful to this promise, although he was quite bored with it all.

In Sunday school he was placed in a class where Edward Kimball was the teacher. One day Mr. Kimball gave Dwight a Bible and told him that the lesson was in John. Moody took the Bible and looked all through the Old Testament for the Gospel of John. When some of the other students saw it, they began to laugh and snicker, but the teacher quickly took the Bible, found the place and gave it to Dwight Moody. From then on, Dwight had the highest respect for his Sunday school teacher, Mr. Kimball.

Mr. Kimball decided that he should speak to Dwight about being a Christian. One day he went to the shoe store where Moody was working. He went to the back room, where Dwight Moody was wrapping shoes. After Mr. Kimball had told him about the love of the Lord Jesus and God's way of salvation, Dwight Moody accepted the Lord Jesus Christ as his own, personal Saviour. Dwight was 18 years old at the time. The first thing he decided to do after he became a Christian was go before the church committee to see if they would let him join the church. He had been in Mr. Kimball's class for only a short time, so he did not know very much about the Word of God.

54

When the committee began to ask him questions, Dwight could not answer them. He did not know too much about the Bible. All he knew was that he had accepted Jesus Christ as his personal Saviour. The committee decided not to let him join; they asked him to study more and come back later. He did this, and this time he was accepted. This was in May, 1856. Dwight Moody never felt bitter toward the committee for not accepting him that first time. He said that he did not blame them, for the church had to know that a person was truly born again before they accepted him. Dwight Moody began to attend the Friday church prayer meetings regularly.

Dwight Moody was not satisfied living in Boston. He decided he wanted to go to Chicago. He wrote his mother about it. While she did not especially care to see him go she, too, believed that God was leading. Dwight had told her that he would give his life to the Lord's service if God would bring him to Chicago.

After he had been in the big city only one week, he wrote to his mother and said, "I went to a prayer meeting last night, and as soon as I made myself known, I had friends. . . . God is the same here as He was in Boston."

Since Dwight had worked in a shoe store in Boston, he soon found work in a shoe store in Chicago. Once more Moody did good work, and soon he was able to write home and say, "I have made $30 a week ever since I came out here." God was blessing Dwight Moody, but He was also preparing him to do something very special.

The first Sunday Moody was in Chicago, he attended the First Baptist Church. There he met a young girl who was later to become his wife.

As D. L. Moody looked around, he realized that there were many young men in this city who were away from their own homes and who were probably a little lonely. So Dwight rented four pews in the church and invited all of these men to attend and sit in his pews. This was the beginning of the special work of Dwight Moody.

Mr. Moody was not satisfied with just renting pews in the church and filling them with people from the streets. He soon joined the Young Men's Mission Band and visited hotels and boarding houses on Sunday mornings, giving out tracts and inviting people to church. One Sunday afternoon he went to a small mission and offered to teach a class in their Sunday school. But the superintendent of the mission said he had too many teachers and not enough pupils. He told Dwight Moody that he could have a class of his own if he wanted to go out and get his own pupils.

The following Sunday Dwight Moody, followed by 18 ragged, dirty children, attended the afternoon Sunday school in the mission. Instead of sitting down and teaching these children, Mr. Moody turned them over to another teacher and went out to find more. He was sure the other people could do a better job of teaching, and he could just go out and find the people who needed to come to the services.

In the fall of 1858, Mr. Moody decided to start his own Sunday school in a place where a saloon had been. In almost no time he was in need of a bigger building. When the mayor of the city found that he was trying to help some of the children, he gave him a building called "North Market Hall." Since this building was used for dances, drinking and smoking late on Saturdays, it was necessary for Mr. Moody to go there at 6:00 Sunday morning to sweep out the beer bottles and cigar stumps and rearrange the furniture for their Sunday school service.

Only a short time passed, and Dwight Moody began to hold Sunday evening services for the boys too. After leading them to Christ, he taught them that they should tell others about their own Christian experience. He told them that they should read God's Word. As he continued to teach the boys, some of the parents became interested and attended the services.

About this time Mr. Moody decided that he could no longer work in business. He must give himself wholly to God's work. He knew this would be a sacrifice, but he could not let money get in the way. The last eight months that he spent in business he made $5000. The first year in Christian work he did not receive more than $300. Sometimes, he admitted, it meant living on crackers and cheese and sleeping on benches, but it was all for the Lord Jesus. From that day on, Dwight Moody became one of God's wonderful workers.

D. L. Moody—God's Evangelist

Dwight L. Moody had been a good shoe salesman, a good Sunday school worker and a good visitor for the Lord. But now God was leading him into full-time Christian work. He gave up his job and began to put all his time into leading people to the Lord Jesus.

In the Sunday night services in North Market Hall, people were accepting Christ as Saviour. Not only were the children coming, the parents were also attending. After they had made their decision for Christ, Moody would suggest that they go to another church. But most of these people came from very poor families and did not enjoy a big, beautiful church. As a result, D. L. Moody decided to build a place that would be used as a church. It would seat about 1500 people. This building was dedicated in 1864 and became one of the most active churches in the city. They had special meetings for men, boys, mothers, and girls. They had Bible meetings, praise services, prayer and testimony meetings and always a special watch night service and a Thanksgiving service. Besides the meetings in the church, they had prayer meetings in the homes and open-air meetings on the streets. God blessed the work of D. L. Moody.

Even in his busy work at the church and Sunday school, D. L. Moody still had time to deal with individuals. One night as he was on his way home, he saw a man leaning against a lamp post. Mr. Moody went up to him and said, "Sir, are you a Christian?"

The man became angry and was just about ready to punch Mr. Moody.

"I am very sorry if I have offended you," said Mr. Moody, "but I thought I was asking a proper question."

"Mind your own business," said the man.

This was Moody's opportunity. He said, "This is my business" and then left the man.

Several months later, there was a knock at Mr. Moody's door. When he opened the door, he saw the man who months before had told him to mind his own business.

"I want to become a Christian," said the man. "I haven't had any peace since that night. Your words have haunted and troubled me. I couldn't get any sleep last night, and I thought I'd come and get you to pray with me." That night Dwight L. Moody led the man to the Lord. He later became a Sunday school teacher in Mr. Moody's church.

D. L. Moody was a good Bible student. He got up early in the morning in order to have two or three hours alone with God and the Bible. He felt this was the time of day to do it because his mind was clear. As Mr. Moody continued to study his Bible, teach his Sunday school class and preach in the church, his popularity grew. He received invitations from different churches to visit them and speak.

In 1867 Mrs. Moody became ill. The doctors suggested that Mr. and Mrs. Moody take a long trip. Since Mr. Moody had always wanted to meet Charles Spurgeon and George Mueller, they decided to take a trip to England. While Mr. Moody was not known to the people there, he did have a chance to preach a few times and also to meet Mr. Spurgeon and Mr. Mueller. The Moodys also visited in Ireland.

After Moody returned to America, he began preaching more than ever. He was invited to speak to many more churches and groups.

One day Mr. Moody met a young man whose name was Ira D. Sankey. He was about 30 years old and worked for the government. He was a very good singer and a very fine song leader. Mr. Moody talked with him and then said, "You will have to give up your government position and come with me. You are the man I have been looking for, for the last eight years."

Mr. Sankey was very surprised but promised to pray about it. Some time later, he joined Mr. Moody in the evangelistic work, helping much in the meetings. Mr. Moody felt that people liked singing and knew that God could use it to reach the people's hearts.

Then came the big Chicago fire in 1871. For a time Dwight L. Moody and Ira D. Sankey were separated. But exactly two months and 15 days after the fire, D. L. Moody conducted the dedication of the new North Side Tabernacle, the building which they had built to take the place of the one that had burned.

After the work at the church was well organized and Mr. Moody felt that he could get away, he decided to take another trip across the sea. Again he went to London and was asked to preach in one of the churches there. In the morning service nothing seemed to happen. In fact, Mr. Moody thought things were very cold, but in the evening service something seemed to come over him, which he did not understand. When he finished his message and gave the invitation, hundreds of people seemed to be standing for prayer. Mr. Moody thought that they did not understand what he said, so he asked only those who really wanted to become Christians to come forward for prayer. All those who were standing went. Mr. Moody followed them into the inquiry room and again wondered if they really knew what he had said. He

60

said that only those who wanted to become Christians should stand. The whole audience stood. These meetings were so wonderful that Mr. Moody returned and held special services for ten days. About 400 people were accepted into the church during that time.

Soon Mr. Moody found the reason for the wonderful services—a woman who was sick in bed had read about Mr. Moody's meetings in America. She had prayed that God would send him to her own church in London, but she had said nothing to anyone else. The morning Mr. Moody came, her sister came home from church and told her that Mr. Moody, from America, had preached.

"God has heard my prayer," said the sick woman, and she spent the rest of the afternoon praying that God would do something very special in the evening service. God heard her prayer, and that evening people came to Christ.

The church asked Mr. Moody to come back the next year. This time he arranged to take Ira D. Sankey with him. They preached and sang the gospel. After five weeks of meetings, several hundred people had come to believe in the Lord Jesus Christ. The chapel, where they began their services, was soon too small to hold the audience, so they rented one of the largest halls in England.

A secular newspaper wrote about the meetings. This was rather unusual, for in those days the newspapers rarely mentioned any religious services. The more the newspaper printed about the meetings, the more invitations came to Dwight L. Moody and Ira D. Sankey for meetings in other places.

One day an invitation came from Edinburgh,

Scotland. Mr. Moody and Mr. Sankey felt that this was of the Lord, so they went to Edinburgh to hold services. So many people attended the meetings that they had to hold three and four meetings, one after the other, to take care of the crowd.

After they had been in Edinburgh for three months, they went to Glasgow. Again God used these men, and many hundreds of people were saved. On the next to the last night of the services, Mr. Moody asked only the people who had accepted Christ during this campaign to attend. At that service 3500 people came. The next night, their closing meeting, there were about 50,000 people in the service.

Moody and Sankey then went to Belfast, Ireland, where big crowds came to hear the gospel of Jesus. After several months of wonderful meetings, the two evangelists returned to London. Since London was such a big city, they knew they would not be able to find one building that would hold all the people who wanted to come. So they held their meetings in the Agricultural Hall in North London, which held about 15,000 or 20,000 people and also in the Royal Opera House, which seated about 5000. In both places there were overflow crowds to hear the 38-year-old evangelist from America.

After these wonderful meetings in London, Moody and Sankey returned to America and held meetings in such cities as New York, Philadelphia, Chicago, Boston and other places. In each case God used these men to begin revivals in the hearts of people. Mr. Sankey not only sang at the services and led the singing but also organized choirs of sometimes 600, 700 and 800 voices to sing the gospel of the Lord Jesus.

God used D. L. Moody, not only in the United States but also in many other countries of the world.

On November 16, 1899, Dwight Lyman Moody preached his last sermon—to some 15,000 people meeting in Convention Hall in Kansas City, Missouri. That night hundreds of people came to the Lord Jesus.

Mr. Moody was sick for just about one month; then on December 22, 1899, God opened the door to heaven and invited Dwight Moody to enter. During his last hours Mr. Moody said to his family, "This is my coronation day. It is glorious."

People came from far and near to attend the funeral of the outstanding evangelist. They could not help but remember something that Mr. Moody had said some years before: "Someday you will read in the papers that D. L. Moody of East Northfield is dead. Don't you believe a word of it. At that moment I shall be more alive than I am now. I shall have gone up higher. That is all."

And that is what he did; he went to be with the Lord Jesus. His earthly work was done, and his Saviour, for whom he had worked, was waiting for him.

Frances Havergal

Frances R. Havergal is best known for writing words and music to songs. Many people who write poems do not write music, but it was different with Frances Havergal. God gave her a gift for both words and music. She has written many of our well-known Sunday school and church songs.

Frances Havergal—God's Faithful Poet

It was in a very fine Christian home in Astley, England, on December 14, 1836, that Frances Ridley Havergal was born. Her father was a pastor, a well-educated man and a fine musician. He composed many songs and hymns.

Frances was an unusual child. When she was only three years old, she was able to read. Often her family would find her sitting, reading a book, when they thought she was out playing.

When "Fanny," as she was called for many years, was four years old, she was able to read the Bible as well as many other books which belonged to her mother and father.

Mr. and Mrs. Havergal realized that their girl was brilliant, for it was soon after her fourth birthday that she learned to write. It seemed no time at all before she was able to learn the French language. They also noticed her interests and abilities in music. This, of course, made her father very happy, for he had hoped that one of his children would carry on his interest in music.

Frances's father had written and sold several hundred songs, but he did not keep the money that he received for them. All of the profits which came from his songs went to the Lord's work.

Even though Frances played some with the neighborhood children, most of her time was spent reading and writing poems. By the time Frances Havergal was seven years old, she had written a book of poems.

Both her mother and her father were godly people. They always had prayer with the family. When Frances Havergal was 11 years old, her mother became very sick and soon passed away. On her deathbed, Mrs. Havergal called Frances to her. She told the little girl to give herself wholeheartedly to the Lord, to give her heart to the Lord Jesus and to turn all of her talents over to Him. Frances was the youngest in the family, and Mrs. Havergal had a special concern for her little girl. Just before Mrs. Havergal passed away, she said, "Remember, nothing but the precious blood of Jesus can make you clean and lovely in God's sight." Frances never forgot those words.

Because Frances was so far advanced in everything, she was not able to attend school with other children. She studied English, German, French, Hebrew, Latin and Welsh at home and was able to read books and pamphlets in all of these languages. When she was 14 years old, she was sent to a girls' school. While she was a student at this school, she made a definite stand for the Lord Jesus and accepted Christ as her Saviour. For the first time in her life she truly realized the cleansing that her mother had talked about.

"It was the word 'cleanseth' which opened the door of hope to me," she said. "Not a coming to be cleansed in the fountain only, but remaining in the fountain so that it may and can go on cleansing."

Now that Frances Havergal had made her decision for Christ, she decided to take a Sunday school class in her father's church. She was only 14, but she was a fine teacher. She kept the names and addresses, the birthdays and something about each child in a book so that she would be able to help the girls whenever they needed her.

When Frances was 16 years old, her father remarried. Because his health was not good, they all moved to Germany. Now Frances attended a German school for girls. She had not been at this school long when she noticed that the students did not care about the Lord Jesus. Instead of being disappointed, Frances took this as a challenge. She made up her mind to be a good witness to them and, if at all possible, win them to the Lord.

Mr. Havergal taught his daughter the Greek language. Very soon she was able to read the entire New Testament in Greek. Besides her studies, she still continued to use much of her time to write poems.

Since Frances Havergal also had musical talent, she put some of her poems to music and submitted them to an outstanding musician, Ferdinand Hiller. Mr. Hiller was so impressed with the words and music she had written that he asked if she would be interested in studying music—so she could know how to write really good music. She did.

Since Frances also had a lovely voice, she was chosen to be the soloist with the Philharmonic Society. This was a real thrill to her. In fact she thought it was one of the most wonderful things that ever happened to her. But as she began to think about it, she wondered if she were forgetting God in it all. This is what she said about it: "A power entirely new and unexpected was given, and rejoicing in this, I forgot the Giver and found such delight in this that other things paled before it. I prayed that if this was hindering me, that the gift of song might be withdrawn."

God answered prayer. Suddenly she became sick and lost her voice. After she had recovered, Frances Havergal began to work with various groups. She gave vocal lessons to people, but she also continued to study voice. Even though she was a busy person, she still continued to write poetry and music. This was a gift which God had given her, and she could not forget it.

One of the most familiar songs Frances Havergal gave us is "Take My Life and Let It Be." It came to her in a rather strange way. One day as she was visiting with some friends in their home, she realized that ten people were there and most of them were not Christians. Many of them had Christian friends and relatives who had prayed for them for a long time. There were a few Christians also, but they did not seem to be happy in the salvation they had. As Frances Havergal thought about these ten people, she prayed, "Lord, give me all in this house."

Frances stayed in this home for five days, and before she left, God had answered her prayer. Every one of those who were not Christians had made a decision for Christ. All of those who had accepted Christ, but who did not seem happy as Christians, came to the Lord and asked Him to take their lives and use them. It was then that Frances Havergal wrote these words:

> Take my life, and let it be
> Consecrated, Lord, to Thee;
> Take my hands, and let them move
> At the impulse of Thy love.
>
> Take my feet, and let them be
> Swift and beautiful for Thee;
> Take my voice, and let me sing,
> Always, only, for my King.
>
> Take my silver and my gold,
> Not a mite would I withhold;
> Take my moments and my days,
> Let them flow in ceaseless praise.
>
> Take my will and make it Thine,
> It shall be no longer mine;
> Take my heart, it is Thine own,
> It shall be Thy royal throne.

Another well-known hymn which Frances Havergal wrote and which you probably often use in your church is "I Gave My Life for Thee." She wrote this song while she was in Germany. One day she saw a motto on the wall under a picture of Christ. It read, "I Gave My Life for Thee." She began to think of these words and soon wrote the poem on a piece of scrap paper. As she read the words over again, she did not think that they were good. The lines did not impress her very much so she crumpled the paper and threw it into the fireplace.

But God was watching over those words. He knew they were something that could be used for His glory, so He kept the paper from falling into the fire. It fell just short of the flame. Frances saw this and decided that God must have something for her in this poem, so she picked it up. Several months later she showed the song to her father. He read the words carefully and told her to be sure to keep them, for God could use them. This poem was put to music by Philip P. Bliss, and you no doubt sing it very often in your church and Sunday school.

Frances learned many lessons from her father, but one of the important lessons was to give her money to the Lord. Whenever Mr. Havergal wrote a song and sold it, he felt that that money belonged to God. Frances seemed to feel the same way. Whenever she received money from her poems, she gave it to God.

Frances Havergal not only wrote poems and hymns and studied and taught voice, she also directed choirs.

In 1873 she became quite sick, so she went to Switzerland to try to regain her health. When she came home again, much to her surprise she found many, many letters waiting for her. They were from all over, most of them from people she did not know. The letters told her that her songs and poems had meant a great deal to them, especially when they were in a time of sorrow or when death had come to someone in the family.

Sometimes people asked Frances Havergal how she could write such lovely poems. She would always say that she could not just sit down and write a poem any time she pleased. All of her inspiration came from the Lord, so she waited on Him.

When God knew that the work of Frances Havergal was finished, when her last poem and her last song had been written, when her last choir had been directed and when her last solo had been sung, He took her home to be with Him. It was on June 3, 1879.

Frances Ridley Havergal was only 42 years old when she went to meet her Saviour, but she left behind some beautiful poems, lovely songs and messages from God. Some of them are "I Am Trusting Thee, Lord Jesus," "Tell It Out Among the Nations" and "Who Is on the Lord's Side?"

John and Betty Stam

John and Betty Stam are best known because they became missionary martyrs—that is, they were killed by enemies because they were preaching about the Lord Jesus. Many years ago missionaries were often martyred, but John and Betty were known as modern martyrs because they were killed in 1934, much more recently than many of the others. They became more famous after their death than before.

John and Betty Stam—Modern Martyrs

John Stam was born in New Jersey. His father's name was Peter Stam. John's father built his own house. He was also in charge of "The Star of Hope" Mission. Both John's mother and father believed on the Lord Jesus. They had asked Jesus to come into their hearts and take away their sin.

John had eight brothers and sisters. These children went to a Christian grammar school.

When John's mother set the table for their meals, she always put a Bible near every plate. Before the family started eating, there was prayer, and then each one took a turn reading verses from

73

the Bible. They did this at every meal, three times a day.

When John was 15 years old, he asked Jesus to come into his heart and be his Saviour. John was a very good student. One day while he was sitting at his desk in school, he told the Lord he wanted to be one of God's workers. Then John began to plan what he would do when he finished high school. He decided that he would go on to Bible school.

After John finished all his studies at high school, he went to the Moody Bible Institute in Chicago. Here he began to prepare for the Lord's work.

The other students at the school liked John very much. They recognized him as a very fine Christian young man, and at the end of his training, the six-foot, two-inch senior was chosen as class speaker, a high honor.

At first John did not know what he would do or where God would send him, but he was willing to be God's worker anywhere.

Betty Scott was born in Michigan. Her father was a Presbyterian minister there. When Betty was only six months old, she and her parents went to China. Betty had four brothers and sisters, but she was the oldest.

After Betty's family had been in China for 17 years, they came to the United States for a furlough. When their furlough time was up, they began to get ready to go back to China. Betty decided to stay in the United States. She wanted to go to college. While Betty was in college in Pennsylvania, she told the Lord she wanted to be in His work. She was sure God would want her to go back to China as a missionary. She had lived there almost all of her life. She knew the people, she knew their ways and she knew their language.

After Betty had finished college, she went to the Moody Bible Institute in Chicago. She started her work there one year before John Stam arrived.

Since Betty was interested in China, she attended the prayer meetings of the China Inland Mission every Monday night. At one of the meetings Betty met this young man named John Stam. John was interested in China too. Week after week they met at the prayer meeting to learn more about China and to help pray for the people there.

Since Betty started her work at the Moody Bible Institute a year before John did, she graduated one year earlier. She and John decided that God wanted her to go to China right away, so she sailed for China. Shortly after she arrived on the field, Betty saw the death of another missionary's baby girl. The baby had been sick. Betty and the mother were taking the child to a hospital, but on their way bandits stopped them. The mother begged the bandits to give her the bag of medicine for her little child. Since she begged for the bag, the bandits decided that there must be something very valuable inside, so they refused. After a long argument the bandits finally gave the mother the bag, but by this time the child was very, very sick. When Betty, the mother and the baby finally managed to get away from the bandits and on to the hospital, it was too late. The little child died.

After this experience Betty realized that missionaries not only had to be willing to give themselves for the work of the Lord, they had to be willing to turn over their children to the Lord too. This made a very deep impression on Betty

75

and was remembered by her even after her own little girl was born.

John stayed at Bible school to finish his studies. It was a whole year later that he arrived in China and began his language study at a mission school in Anking.

The Communists were at work in China, and it seemed to the missionaries in that area that more and more problems were coming to the front.

On October 25, 1933, when John had finished his first year of study of the Chinese language, he and Betty were married by Rev. Reuben A. Torrey, son of the famous evangelist, Dr. R. A. Torrey. Besides the missionaries, some 140 Chinese Christians attended Betty's and John's wedding. In Chinese weddings the bride never looks up at the groom; in fact, she does not smile or look pleasant. So the Chinese Christians realized right away that Betty and John were very happy, for as Betty came down the aisle, her eyes were on John and on her lips was a beautiful smile.

For their honeymoon John and Betty went back to the place where Betty had spent her childhood. Then they came to Suancheng to begin their work together. They worked there for almost one year; then, on September 11, 1934, God gave John and Betty Stam a beautiful baby girl. They named her Helen Priscilla.

All this time the Communists were at work. The missionaries often found it hard to continue their work in China, but they asked God to help them.

One day John and Betty Stam received the warning that some Communist soldiers were coming. At first they did not know what to do, for their baby was only three months old. They called the servants together, and then all of them knelt for prayer. In just a few minutes the soldiers pounded on their front door. John and Betty opened it. They were very kind to the soldiers. Betty even served them tea and cakes. But in spite of this, the soldiers were very cruel. They told John and Betty to give them all their money. John and Betty obeyed. Then they took John and tied a rope around him and took him away to the Communist headquarters.

It was not long until they released John and he was able to go back to his home again but only for a short time. The soldiers came again. This time they took all three of them—John, Betty and little Helen Priscilla. One of the villagers saw what was happening. He cried, "Don't harm an innocent baby like this." This made the Communist officer very angry. He decided that either the baby must die or somebody must give his life for the child.

"Who will forfeit his life for the child?" the officer cried angrily. The man from the village offered his life, and in a moment he was killed. He had given his life for little Helen Priscilla Stam.

On December 7, 1934, John and Betty gave their lives too. One of the soldiers had a sword in his hand. With a quick motion he struck John Stam, and the missionary fell dead. Then he turned and with another quick motion with the same sword took the life of Betty Stam.

Together John and Betty Stam had served the Lord, though for just a short time. Together they had gone to be with the Lord Jesus. They had given their lives for the sake of the gospel.

In a little house not too far away Helen Priscilla had been left alone for more than 24 hours. She could not know what had happened. At first no one dared to go near the house. The Chinese were afraid the Communists would be watching. Later a brave Chinese pastor made his way into the house and snatched the baby into his arms. She was still in her sleeping bag, warm and unharmed. It was not long until her grandparents, Dr. and Mrs. Scott (Betty's mother and father), were located, and little Helen Priscilla was sent to live with them.

John and Betty Stam were young when they died—only 27 and 28—but their work for the Lord Jesus was ended. They had obeyed God's call. We should obey God's call too.

Betty's favorite Bible verse was Philippians 1:21: "For to me to live is Christ, and to die is gain." She often said, "By life, or by death" (v. 20). She wanted to be a worker for the Lord.

John Bunyan

John Bunyan is best known for having written a book, *Pilgrim's Progress*. This book tells about a character whose name is Christian. It tells how Christian came to know the Lord and tells about his walk in the Christian life. Another thing which made John Bunyan famous was the fact that this book was written while he was in prison. He was put there for preaching about Jesus.

John Bunyan—Writer

Most Christian biographies (stories about the lives of men and women) tell about important people—preachers, singers and missionaries—who did great things for God.

This is not true of this story. This is about a man who did not even know God until after he was married. But then later on John Bunyan wrote one of the greatest books ever to be written—*Pilgrim's Progress*.

His book has been translated into more than a hundred languages and has also been rewritten for children and young people.

John Bunyan was born in Bedford, England, in November, 1628. He did not have a Christian home. His mother and father did not believe in God.

John's great-great-grandfather was not a very good man. He and John's great-great-grandmother had a small roadside inn (a hotel). Since they were not Christians, they did many things that were not right. Twelve different times these people were arrested and fined for charging their customers too much money.

John's grandfather was a tinker—a person who sold and repaired all kinds of pots, pans and kettles. Grandfather Bunyan traveled all over the country, going from house to house selling and mending pots and pans. When John's father grew up, he did the same thing. He followed in the business of his father, as this was the custom. Because it was the custom, John Bunyan also sold and repaired pots and pans when he grew up.

While we do not know much about the early life of John Bunyan, we do know that he came from a poor family and a family that was not Christian. John did not have much of an education. He had just learned to read and write when he quit school to go to work and help earn food for the family.

John did not grow up to be a good boy. He had many hours with nothing special to do, so he was led into mischief. He began to lie, swear and cheat and did not seem to respect any of his elders. But there was one thing in which John was very good. It was sports. He was one of the best athletes in his community.

80

Because John was so often unhappy at home, he decided to join the army when he was 16 years old. John was a soldier for more than two years. For awhile he did not seem to care if he lived or died. Both his mother and his sister had died by this time, and he did not think there was much to live for. But God knew that some day John Bunyan could be needed in His work, so He took care of him in the army.

One time John was ordered to go with the army to make an attack. This would be very dangerous and would probably take his life. Just before they were to leave, another man was chosen to go in his place. This man was killed in the battle. When John heard this, he began to think very seriously. Perhaps there was a reason why he had been spared. It was not long, however, before he forgot about this narrow escape and was once again living an ungodly life.

Sometimes John would dream about eternal things. When he awakened he would decide never to sin. But in just a matter of minutes, he would forget about the promise he made and go right back into sin. John knew he was a sinner. He knew that cheating, swearing and lying were sin, but he just could not seem to change.

When John Bunyan was 19 years old, he married. His wife came from a fine Christian home. She learned to know about God at an early age. So, very often as John and his wife were in their home, she would talk to him about God.

While John did not remember very much from his reading and writing lessons in school, she encouraged and helped him to read some books that her father had given them. She also reminded him in a very kind way that he needed to become a Christian. Often John Bunyan would try to "turn over a new leaf" and become religious, thinking that this would be enough. He even went to church twice every Sunday with his wife. He stopped swearing; he tried to drop one sinful thing after another, until he was sure he was living a very good life. Many of the people who knew him saw that there was a change. But in spite of all this, he had not really changed, for he had not given his heart to God. He had changed things in his outward life, but that was all.

John kept selling pots and pans and mending the kettles that were broken. One day, while he went through the streets, calling "Pots and pans to mend, pots and pans to mend," he saw three ladies. He could tell that they were poor, but there was something about them that caught his attention. It was the way they were talking. They were talking about the Lord Jesus Christ.

John had never believed that one could be religious and still be happy, but as he talked to these women, he learned that things could be so different. They explained to him that it was not changing his way that would make him a Christian. They told him of the love of God, how God gave His Son, the Lord Jesus, to die for him. That day, for the first time, John Bunyan heard the true gospel of the Lord Jesus.

After he had talked to these women, John decided to go home and read the Bible. He began to read it regularly and also went to talk to the women just as often as he could. Sometimes he would ask them questions they could not answer.

When this happened, they would tell him to go to a man by the name of Mr. Gifford.

The more John Bunyan read the Bible, the more he talked with these women, and the more he asked Mr. Gifford, the more he realized that he was a very guilty sinner. Often he would go up to the attic of his little house and cry and pray to God. Sometimes he thought he had committed so many sins that God could never forgive him.

One day John Bunyan became sick. How discouraged he was! All he could think of was that his heart was full of sin. During this sickness John Bunyan read a book by Martin Luther. Then it was not long until John Bunyan gave his heart and life to the Lord Jesus and became one of God's own children.

Because John Bunyan became a Christian did not mean that he did not have problems. In that year of 1655 John Bunyan had many sorrows. First, his dear friend, Rev. John Gifford, the man who had helped him so much, died. After a short time his wonderful wife also died. Then John became sick, and he was very near death, but God spared him.

John Bunyan thought that the death of his wife was almost more than he could take. But he found that the Lord Jesus, his Saviour, could be his true helper.

Now that John Bunyan's life belonged to God, he decided to do something for God while selling his pots and pans. As he went from house to house selling and mending his wares, he also told people about the Lord Jesus Christ. God even blessed John Bunyan's business so that he was able to sell and mend more than he had ever done before. He was able to tell more people about the Lord too.

But in those days there was a law in England that said no one except a minister could preach. Even though this was a law, John Bunyan knew that God's Word said, "Go ye into all the world, and preach the gospel to every creature" (Mark 16:15). John decided that it was best to obey God, so he kept right on preaching while he was mending pots and pans.

In 1659 John Bunyan married again. This girl's name was Elizabeth. She was a very brave woman and was a real help to her husband. She took care of John's four children, and she encouraged him to continue his preaching.

Then came a change in the leadership of England, and new laws were made. One law said that if anyone except an ordained minister preached, he would be thrown into prison and severely punished. John Bunyan did not want to go against the law of his country, and yet he knew that it was better to obey God than man. For a while he dressed in strange costumes in order to change his looks and sneak out to places of preaching. But soon he decided this was not the way to preach the gospel, so he went out boldly. One day John Bunyan was asked to come to a nearby village to preach. He promised. His friends told him that police officers knew he was going there and would try to stop him. John Bunyan knew that God would be there, too, so he went.

As he began his sermon, a policeman walked up and arrested him and then took him to the Justice of the Peace. John Bunyan was told that he could go free if he would promise not to preach again.

But this was something John Bunyan could not promise. Perhaps he remembered how the Apostle Peter had been told the same thing many years before.

When John Bunyan's trial came up, he was not allowed to speak. He was not allowed to bring in any witnesses to defend him. He was pronounced guilty and put into prison. His sentence stated that he would be imprisoned for three months. After that time if he promised never to preach again, they would release him. If he would not make the promise, they would have to hang him. Imagine— hanging a man because he preached about the Lord Jesus!

Finally, after sentence had been passed, Mr. Bunyan was given the chance to talk. His words were, "If I were out of prison today, I would preach again tomorrow, so help me, God."

John Bunyan's imprisonment was not over in three months. It continued for 12 long years. He could have been released from prison any time during those 12 years if he had only promised not to preach about the Lord Jesus again. But John Bunyan loved the Lord, and he knew that he had to preach about Him, even though it meant prison, separation from his wife and children and not being able to support them in any way. John Bunyan loved his home. His business of mending pots and pans had grown. He loved the out-of-doors, the air, the sunshine, the grass, the blue sky. But in spite of all this, John Bunyan chose to spend 12 years in prison because he loved the Lord and wanted to serve Him.

The prison was dirty, dark, crowded and full of sickness. Some prisoners died as a result of those conditions. At times there were as many as 50 men crowded together in one small room. Some of them were murderers or other criminals, while others were there because they did not attend the State church and wanted to preach as they were led by the Lord Jesus.

In a short time John Bunyan realized that he could preach to his fellow prisoners. This he did, and many of them joined with him for prayer regularly.

Though his 12-year imprisonment was hard on John Bunyan, he did not waste any of his time. He made use of every minute, reading God's Word, praying and writing. It was here that he wrote his famous book, *Pilgrim's Progress*.

At the age of 43 John Bunyan was finally released from prison. He was asked to become the pastor of the Baptist Church in Bedford. He accepted and was the pastor for the next 16 years. However, he not only preached in this one church but went to many other places, such as London and Cambridge. He preached to the university students and at street meetings and sometimes in an old building. Even though he was threatened many times, he was not put into prison again for his preaching.

John Bunyan was often called on to help in home and family problems. One day a boy who lived in Mr. Bunyan's neighborhood ran away from home. After some time the boy decided to come back, but by this time the parents had decided not to let him return. The boy asked John Bunyan if he would help him get back into his parents' home. Mr. Bunyan talked to the parents, who promised to take their boy back once more. John Bunyan decided he would go and bring the boy home. For 40 miles on the trip it rained so hard that John Bunyan was chilled and fevered by the time he got there. As a result he became very sick and on August 31, 1688, at the age of 59, John Bunyan went to be with his Saviour.

So the author of one of the world's greatest books, *Pilgrim's Progress*, finished his work, but his book still remains. It will probably remain for years and years to come.

Ira D. Sankey

Ira D. Sankey is best known for having written so many gospel songs and hymns. He is also known because he was the song leader for the D. L. Moody evangelistic meetings. Another thing that made him famous was his wonderful voice. People would come from far and near to hear him sing.

Ira D. Sankey—Singer of Sermons

In II Timothy 3:15 we read: "From a child thou hast known." Not only did Ira David Sankey learn the Scriptures from his mother and father, but the first hymns that he memorized were those he heard his mother singing to him when he was a very small boy.

On cold winter evenings the Sankeys, with their nine children, would sit around the log fireplace and sing the old hymns. David, as he was called, loved the old songs. When he was eight years old, he could read music well enough to sing many of the old, familiar hymns.

When David was 17 years old, his father was made the president of the bank. David went to high school and had many educational opportunities that some boys of his day were not able to have.

Just a short time before David began high school, he accepted the Lord Jesus as his Saviour. In his church he was a real leader. He directed the choir, became a soloist and was made the superintendent of the Sunday school and a teacher of a class. He studied the lessons carefully to be sure he would be able to answer any questions his class might ask.

At the age of 20 Ira D. Sankey enlisted in the army. There he continued to sing and even helped the chaplain by leading the singing in the religious services at the camp. Many evenings the men would sit around and listen to him give them the gospel in song.

In 1863 Mr. Sankey married a young lady who had sung in his church choir. God gave them three very fine boys.

While working with the Young Men's Christian Association (YMCA), David had a chance to sing at conventions, conferences, churches and even political gatherings. He always sang gospel songs and never accepted money for singing.

On one occasion he attended a YMCA convention in Indianapolis. He heard that D. L. Moody was to speak at a certain prayer meeting, so he went to the service. During the service David began to sing the familiar hymn, "There Is a Fountain Filled With Blood." At the close of this service, D. L. Moody stopped to ask him what type of work he was doing. Mr. Sankey told him that he was a government employee. To this Mr. Moody said, "You will have to give it up. I've been looking for you for eight years."

Ira D. Sankey was not sure if he should give up his job or not. Then Mr. Moody asked to meet him on a certain corner at a certain time. When Ira D. Sankey got there, Mr. Moody set a box before him and told him to stand on it and sing. Sankey started to sing and in just a short time there was a crowd. Then Moody began to preach. More and more people came, so Mr. Moody told them to go to the opera building and the meeting would continue. In minutes the big building was packed. Before long, Ira D. Sankey decided to give up his government job and join Mr. Moody in his meetings.

While in Chicago these two men spent the days visiting the sick and holding noon prayer meetings and the evenings conducting great mass meetings.

On a certain Sunday evening, D. L. Moody and Ira D. Sankey were holding a meeting in Chicago when they heard the sound of scores of fire trucks. This was the big Chicago fire of October 8, 1871. The meeting was quickly dismissed, and people ran to their homes and other places to get away from the fire.

Ira D. Sankey and D. L. Moody were separated. Mr. Sankey spent all of that night out in the middle of Lake Michigan watching, from a small rowboat, the destruction of the big city. Two and one-half months passed before the two men were brought together again. Then their meetings in Chicago started again. This time Sankey and Moody had no place to stay, so they slept together in a corner of the tabernacle where the cold winds and snow often drifted in.

A musician friend of Ira. D. Sankey's offered him a full-time position with a very good salary, if he would travel with him and sing at concerts. If Mr. Sankey had not been a consecrated Christian, he would probably have been tempted to take this new work. But Ira D. Sankey knew that his life belonged to God, so he decided to stay with D. L. Moody and preach the gospel in song.

Even though these two men were very different, God used their work. Mr. Moody's sermons often shocked and startled his listeners, while Mr. Sankey's songs soothed and comforted the people who heard him.

Ira D. Sankey went with Mr. Moody on his trip to Europe where many people came to the services and believed on Christ. While they were holding one evangelistic meeting, another invitation would come to them. In this way, the Moody-Sankey team traveled from country to country, singing and speaking the Word of God. There was very little time left for rest, but these men continued because they had put God first and wanted to win people to the Lord Jesus.

At Northfield, Massachusetts, Mr. Sankey first sang in America his song "The Ninety and Nine." How people loved this song! And how Mr. Sankey enjoyed singing it!

D. L. Moody surely chose a gifted man to be his helper, for Ira D. Sankey not only sang with a beautiful voice, he was always careful to sing the words in a way that everyone could understand what he was singing. He wanted to be able to make his songs sermons so that people would turn to the Lord Jesus and be saved. He knew he could do this if he was very careful to pronounce each word clearly.

Sometimes while Sankey was singing, people

would cry; sometimes they would be glad and thankful, but always they were blessed. After hearing him sing one day, someone said, "That is the most eloquent [expressive] sermon I have ever heard."

Often famous men, such as President Grant, several senators and members of the Supreme Court, would attend the meetings and hear Mr. Sankey sing.

Among the close friends of Mr. and Mrs. Sankey was Fanny J. Crosby, the blind poet who wrote so many sacred songs and hymns. For many years this blind lady spent her summers with the Sankeys at Northfield, Massachusetts. Very often Mr. Sankey would compose the tune to which Fanny Crosby had written the words.

Some of Mr. Sankey's well-known numbers are "Why Not Tonight?" "Welcome, Wanderer, Welcome" and "I Am Praying for You." These songs were used in the revival services of the Moody-Sankey team, and they are still used in meetings today.

After the death of Mr. Moody, Mr. Sankey wrote the song, "Out of the Shadow Land" and sang it at the funeral of his beloved friend and Christian co-worker. This is one of the few songs to which he wrote both words and music.

While Ira D. Sankey was holding special services of sacred song in some of the cities of Great Britain, his health broke, and he lost his eyesight. The man who had brought such light and happiness to hundreds of people spent the rest of his life in physical darkness. It was then that his friend Fanny Crosby, the blind poet, became even more of a blessing and help to Mr. Sankey.

Ira D. Sankey, singer of sermons, went to be with the Lord on August 13, 1908. Even though his beautiful, clear, baritone voice was never to be heard again, his wonderful songs, such as "A Shelter in the Time of Storm," "Hiding in Thee" and "Under His Wings," are still being sung.

Someone has said that there must have been a grand reunion when Mr. Moody and Mr. Sankey met in heaven.

Mary Slessor

Mary Slessor is best known because of her missionary work in Africa. She was not afraid of anything; she knew that God had sent her to that country and that He would take care of her. She not only taught the people better ways to live but also taught them the way to God.

Mary Slessor—White Mother of Africa

Mary Slessor was born in Scotland. Her mother was a lovely Christian woman who prayed to God, but her father was a drunkard. He drank so much that when he did find a good job, he would soon lose it. This made things hard for Mrs. Slessor, Mary and the six other children. Sometimes they went hungry because Mr. Slessor had used the family money for drink.

Because of home conditions, Mary Slessor had to go out and get a job when she was only 11 years old. She found a job at a weaving mill. By the time she was 14, she had become an expert weaver.

Even though she worked hard all day, Mary decided she wanted an education, so she went to school at night. She also read many books. Most of these came from the Sunday school library. She especially loved to read the story of David Livingstone and his experiences in Africa.

Even when Mary was a little girl, she had started thinking about Africa. She was sure that God was talking to her about going there as a missionary. One day she mentioned it to her mother. Since her mother was a praying woman, she told Mary that she thought her girl would someday make a very fine worker for God.

One day a missionary from Africa came to speak in the church where Mary and her mother attended. His message stirred Mary's heart. After she had listened to his testimony, Mary said, "I am going to be a missionary when I grow up."

About this time Mary Slessor began to teach a Sunday school class in a small mission. This mission was located in a very tough neighborhood, and sometimes she was almost mobbed before reaching the mission. However, by the time she got to her class, which consisted of both boys and girls, she forgot the mobbing and talked to them about the Lord Jesus.

Mary Slessor loved these children very much. One day she told them that someday she would leave them and go to Africa as a missionary. She asked the children to pray for her. The children in Mary's Sunday school class became very interested and often talked to her about Africa. They asked her if she was afraid of the snakes and other wild animals in that country. Mary always told her class that she was not afraid, because God would take care of her.

Not too long after this Mary applied to the mission board and was accepted to be a missionary.

She was first sent to another city for special training, which lasted three months. As she was preparing to go, she realized that she would be leaving her mother and the other children alone. When she talked with her mother about it, her mother said, "I willingly let you go; you will make a fine missionary, and I am sure God will be with you."

After three months of special training, Mary boarded a ship and started for Africa. As she looked around on the ship, she saw many barrels of whisky which were being shipped to the dark-skinned people of Africa. This made Mary Slessor stop and think. Many barrels of whisky but on the same ship only one missionary! Having come from a home where her father was a drunkard, Mary knew what this would mean to the poor people of Africa. How she wanted to tell them about the Lord Jesus!

When Mary Slessor finally arrived in the dark continent, she soon found out why it had been given this name. The people were blinded by sin; they did not know the Lord Jesus as Saviour.

The first thing Mary had to do when she arrived in Africa was to learn the language of the people. It was a different language than she had spoken in Scotland. After she had learned the language fairly well, Mary organized a Sunday school class. This class was very different from the one she had had in Scotland. For one thing, there all the boys and girls were white; in Africa all the children were black.

Mary was thrilled with the country. She walked through the forests around her and enjoyed the green grass wherever she found it. But she soon found that there were many bad things in Africa

97

too. In the jungles and in the waters were animals that would be ready to tear her limb from limb. But she had told her Sunday school class that God would care for her. She knew He would not only protect her from the wild animals but also keep her from contacting any of the jungle diseases.

Mary knew that she had to do something to show these people her love for them. She decided that living just exactly as the natives lived would be the answer. Since they wore no shoes, she wore no shoes. She ate whatever food the natives ate, drank the water they drank, slept on the ground as they did.

Early every morning Mary would get up, leave her little house and take some medicine and her Bible to the people. Whenever they were sick, she would try to help them. She would always talk to them about Jesus.

The African people learned to love Mary Slessor. Many of them called her "White Mother." One day when she was talking, one of the men said, "White Mother, do not walk along the riverbanks or you be suddenly snatched by the big jaws and sharp teeth of an alligator." She was glad that they tried to help and protect her.

Up to this time Mary Slessor had worked in a place called Duke Town. But now she felt that God wanted her to go to another village. She felt that God was calling her to work in Okoyong. But the people of Duke Town told her not to go. They said it was a very bad place. They told her that both the people and the animals were wild and dangerous.

"They may make you their prisoner, and you will never come back to us," said some of her native friends. Others told her that the people of

Okoyong would never listen to her. But Mary Slessor knew that God wanted her to go there. He would take care of her. He would make the people listen to her words from the Bible.

When the chief of Duke Town saw that she really wanted to go to Okoyong, he gave her a canoe. He even told his men to go with her and paddle the boat upstream for her. Bravely, Mary Slessor went to Okoyong. There she told the people that their idols were not good. She told them there was only one God. The people of Okoyong were so surprised that Mary Slessor was not afraid of them that they stopped everything they were doing and listened.

These people were fighting people, but Mary Slessor told them that they had to stop fighting and that they should listen to God's Book as she read it to them. Many of these dangerous and cruel men stopped their fighting and listened to all that Mary Slessor had to tell them, and many of them even believed in her God.

Mary was not afraid of hard work. Alone she built a little hut. It was not long until Mary was able to help the people in their work. She showed the men how to work in the fields. She showed the women how to make nice dresses and how to starch their clothing. All of the people enjoyed Mary Slessor's cooking.

But Mary Slessor had her problems too. One day a native warrior came to Mary's house. In his hand he held a rifle. The White Mother told him to put it away, but he refused. Quick as a flash she snatched the gun from his hand and put it in the corner of her room. The man was so surprised that he walked away from the missionary's house like a scolded puppy.

Another time while Mary Slessor was in her house, she saw a group of natives charging down the jungle path. They were on their way to attack a nearby village.

"Stop!" shouted Mary, running out and stepping right in their tracks. Again surprise took the people, and no harm was done to the nearby village.

In the dark continent of Africa, parents were and are even now plagued with superstition. They thought if a mother had twins that it was of the Devil, and they would murder one of the babies. One day Mary found a twin that had been left for dead. She took the baby into her home. She cared for it and loved it. After some time another child was brought to her and another and another. Soon Mary had adopted five orphan children.

One of Mary's closest friends was the chief's sister. Mary learned much from her. The people thought so much of Mary Slessor that even when they had problems so serious that they were ready to kill men, women and children, they would call her to come and settle them.

The British government recognized the good work that Mary Slessor was doing. People no longer seemed to want to kill; they were beginning to live a more peaceful life. Mary's wonderful Christian life had made them stop their life of cannibalism.

"This White Mother is changing our lives," said the people of Okoyong after Mary Slessor had been there for some time. "Instead of war chants, we are singing Christian hymns. Instead of fighting, we are learning to read."

Mary Slessor continued her work with the people of Okoyong until she felt that many of them had been reached with the gospel. Then she went on to another village in the jungle. There she met savages, and again she told these people about Jesus. She stayed until many had been led to Jesus. Then she went on to another new village in the jungle where she found more people who did not know about Christ. Mary continued to go from village to village, telling all the people about the true God and using medicines to make sick people well.

One day when Mary Slessor was in her canoe, going up the river, a huge hippopotamus suddenly attacked her. Quickly she took some pots and pans that were in the boat and slammed them at the big hippopotamus. The hippopotamus went off without harming the missionary.

God took care of her every time. He kept her from the fighting natives. He kept her from the cruel warriors. He kept her from the wild animals.

Most missionaries who go to a faraway country have a furlough. This is a time for them to leave their work and come home for a rest. Mary Slessor had a furlough too. She returned to her home in Scotland. But before she left, she wondered what she could do with all the little black children who were living with her. After much work, she finally found homes for all but four of them. When she could not find a place for these four to stay, she decided to take them with her. When she arrived in Scotland, the people were very surprised to see her with the little black children. At first they did not know what to think of it, but it was not long before they loved the children as much as Mary did.

After her furlough Mary Slessor returned to Africa. She read and taught the Bible to these people. She visited the sick. She helped to build new churches.

After Mary had worked with the people of Africa, many had accepted Christ as Saviour. In fact, there were so many that she had to send for a minister to come and be their pastor.

Finally, after many years of hard work, Mary became very sick. When she was on her deathbed, she had a wonderful nurse. It was one of the little twins whom she had rescued many years before. On January 15, 1914, Mary Slessor went to be with the Lord Jesus.

When the natives were told that their White Mother had gone to be with Jesus in heaven, they were very sad. They wondered how they could get along without her. But Mary Slessor had told them about Jesus, the Saviour. She had helped them to become Christians and to go to church. She had also helped them to read. So, even though she was gone, they could still read God's Book and learn more about Mary Slessor's Saviour.

"Thank you, thank you!" the people of Africa said, for they were all very glad for everything Mary Slessor had done for them.

Fanny Crosby

Fanny Crosby is best known for her wonderful poems. She wrote thousands of them, and many were put to music by different people. Another thing which makes Fanny Crosby well known is the fact that she was blind while she did all this. Some of the best-known songs and hymns used in our churches today were written by Fanny Crosby.

Fanny Crosby—Blind Poet

On March 24, 1820, Frances Jane Crosby was born in a humble home. Her parents were poor. Before "Fanny," as she was called, was a year old, her father died. Mrs. Crosby was left alone to work and take care of her family.

When Fanny was only six weeks old, she became quite sick. Through this sickness her eyes became very weak. At that time they did not have doctors and medicines such as we have, so Fanny Crosby soon became blind.

When little Fanny was old enough to understand, Mrs. Crosby explained the blindness to her. She told her that God sometimes took away one gift in order to give us a better one. She told the

103

little girl about other blind people, some of whom became famous. In this way, Fanny was never bitter about her blindness.

When Fanny Crosby was only eight years old, she wrote her first poem. It was about her blindness:

O, what a happy soul am I!
Although I cannot see,
I am resolved that in this world
Contented I will be.

How many blessings I enjoy,
That other people don't.
To weep and sigh because I'm blind,
I cannot, and I won't.

Fanny Crosby's mother wanted to help her little girl as much as she could. She wanted to take her out and tell her how everything looked. She wanted to become "eyes" for her. But she couldn't. Now that there was no father to go to work and buy food, Fanny's mother had to go to work. So Mrs. Crosby could not spend much time with her girl.

Fanny's grandmother lived with them, so she decided to become Fanny's eyes. She took Fanny up on her lap and told her of the sun. She explained how it looked in the morning. She told how it looked at noon and again just before it went down. She talked to Fanny about the beautiful fluffy clouds in the sky and told her how they kept changing their shapes and forms. Then she explained God's beautiful moon. She told her about each star.

One day after a storm Fanny's grandmother took her to the top of a hill. There she explained and described the beautiful rainbow. She told about the seven colors God had put into the rainbow. She even told her why God had first put the rainbow in the sky.

Grandmother also helped Fanny to tell the difference between the various birds and bird calls. Together they would go into the woods and listen to the birds. Grandmother taught her how to listen for sounds.

Fanny and her grandmother also gave much time to the study of flowers. Fanny could soon tell which was which just by touching and smelling them. How she loved flowers!

But best of all, Fanny's grandmother taught the Bible to the blind girl. Since Fanny could not see to read the verses in the Bible, Grandmother helped her to memorize. She learned many of the verses you now learn in Sunday school. She knew many of the Psalms, the Proverbs and the whole Book of Ruth by heart. She knew almost all of the Old Testament stories and could tell them in detail. Because of this, Fanny Crosby was able to say, "All that I am and all that I expect to be . . . is due to the Bible." Many of the poems she first wrote were the result of hearing the beautiful Bible stories.

Grandmother encouraged Fanny to play with other children. Soon she was able to do almost everything they did. She climbed trees, rode horseback and played other games with them.

It was not until Fanny was 15 years old that she was able to attend the Institution for the Blind

105

in New York City. Here she was to spend 23 wonderful years as a student and as a teacher.

At this school Fanny began to write more poetry. At first teachers and friends discouraged her. Then one day a doctor came to examine all the blind students. When he examined Fanny Crosby, he said, "And here is a poet. Give her every possible encouragement. You will hear from this young lady someday."

Of course, Fanny Crosby was thrilled to hear this. She had felt for a long time that hymnwriting was to be her life work. All she needed was someone to encourage her in it. What the doctor had said was all she needed.

A young man named Grover Cleveland was the superintendent at the New York Institute for the Blind while Fanny was there. When she was 16, Mr. Cleveland helped Fanny by copying all of her poems for her. How happy she was when many years later Grover Cleveland became the president of the United States!

Fanny often visited different churches in New York. Here she would recite some of the poems she had written. She was always glad when she could do this. But a bigger thrill came to Fanny Crosby one day. She was asked to visit Congress. Here a number of her poems were read. As the congressmen listened to the poems, they had to wipe away their tears.

As a result of this visit, Fanny Crosby made many new friends. She knew a number of the United States presidents, some great musicians and some of the great religious leaders. All of them turned out to be her very best friends.

Although Fanny Crosby had always been a very religious person, it was not until she was 31 years old that she accepted the Lord Jesus as her own personal Saviour. From that day on, her poems seemed to mean even more to her than before.

When Fanny Crosby was 38 years old, she met a man named Alexander Van Alstyne. He was blind, too, and he was also at the Institution for the Blind. He was a singer and often sat down and sang beautiful songs to Fanny Crosby. They were married and lived together very happily for 44 years, when Mr. Van Alstyne died. God gave Fanny a little baby. But she did not have this little one very long because the baby soon went to be with Jesus. This is when Fanny Crosby wrote one of her well-known songs, "Safe in the Arms of Jesus."

After studying at the institution for 12 years, Fanny Crosby was asked to stay on as a teacher. She did and taught there for 11 more years.

Fanny Crosby wrote many poems while she was there, yet it was not until after she left the Institution for the Blind that she really became famous because of her songs.

God had given Fanny Crosby a very good memory. This was proved when as a child she memorized so many verses from the Bible. It was also proved one day when she was asked to write some 40 poems. Instead of writing them down one at a time, she worked out each of the 40 poems in her mind. When they were exactly the way she thought they should be, she sat down and wrote all 40 of them on paper.

This gifted poet was always busy. When she wasn't writing, she was working in churches or missions. One night while Fanny was visiting a group of working men at a mission, she talked to them about Jesus, trying hard to make them realize that there was some mother's boy present who had to be rescued that night or be lost forever. A young man about 18 years old came forward, and Fanny Crosby prayed with him and led him to the Lord. In her room later that night, the words of the great hymn "Rescue the Perishing" came to her, and then the next morning they were copied down for music.

One of the most beautiful of all consecration hymns was written by Fanny Crosby after talking to Dr. William H. Doane about the nearness of God. Late that evening she wrote "I Am Thine, O Lord," otherwise known as "Draw Me Nearer."

Ira D. Sankey, the singer in the Moody-Sankey revivals, was a big help in making Fanny Crosby's music known, as he often used her songs in the services. He found the song "Blessed Assurance" a real favorite in the meetings and often closed the meetings with her song, "Pass Me Not, O Gentle Saviour." Some time later when Mr. Sankey became ill he, too, lost his eyesight, and Fanny Crosby often went to visit and comfort him. Together the two blind workers for the Lord sang the hymns which the one had written and the other had carried around the world.

One of Fanny Crosby's truest friends was blind and deaf Helen Keller. Of Miss Keller, Fanny said, "She is one of the greatest gifts to this age."

Because of her great love for children, Fanny Crosby was soon given the name "Aunt Fanny" by all the children in the neighborhood. They included her in their games, told her of their joys and

108

came to her for comfort. Several times a day she would hear a child say, "Please, Aunt Fanny, tell me a story." It was because of this that she wrote the song, "Tell Me the Story of Jesus."

Fanny Crosby knew of the heartbreak and sorrow of this world, but she held fast to one of her favorite Bible verses: "No good thing will he withhold from them that walk uprightly" (Ps. 84:11). Through this she wrote a song that we now know as "Take the World but Give Me Jesus."

On the evening of her 90th birthday, Aunt Fanny spoke to a group of her friends. When asked what the secret of her long life was, she told them it was guarding three things: her temper, her taste and her tongue.

Almost all of her hymns were thought out carefully at night when she was alone. In the morning she would recite them to a typist, who copied them for her.

On February 11, 1915, Fanny Crosby dictated a letter to a friend who had just lost her daughter. Little did she know that this would be her very last writing. During the night Fanny Crosby went to be with the Lord Jesus. Long before the funeral service began, the church was filled. Ministers, songwriters, politicians, statesmen, boys and girls—all of them Fanny's friends—were there. Many of her hymns were sung and, of course, among them the song, "Safe in the Arms of Jesus."

Fanny Crosby's ambitions had been to live long and to have a useful life. Both of these ambitions were reached, for Fanny Crosby was 95 years old when she died, and today we are still singing hundreds of her more than 8000 published hymns.

another book in this series

CHRISTIANS WITH COURAGE

RUTH JOHNSON JAY

Add to your library more biographies of great Christians of the past.

Read about the challenging lives of Hudson Taylor, Martin Luther, Charles Spurgeon and 11 others.

$1.25 each   1724-7

Back to the Bible Broadcast
Box 82808, Lincoln, Nebraska 68501 or
Box 10, Winnipeg, Manitoba R3C 2G2